The Early Books of
Yehuda Amichai

The Early Books of
Yehuda Amichai

THE SHEEP MEADOW PRESS
Riverdale-on-Hudson, New York

This book is published in arrangement with Harper and Row, Inc.

Library of Congress Cataloging-in-Publication Data

Amichai, Yehuda.
  The early books of Yehuda Amichai.

  Contents: Songs of Jerusalem and myself /
translated by Harold Schimmel—Poems / translated
by Ted Hughes and Assia Gutmann—Time.
  1. Jerusalem—Poetry. 2. Amichai, Yehuda—
Translations, English. I. Schimmel, Harold.
II. Hughes, Ted, 1930– . III. Gutmann, Assia.
IV. Title.
PJ5054.A65A27   1988   892.4'16   88-13973
ISBN 0-935296-75-1

Printed in the United States of America.

Contents

Songs of Jerusalem and Myself

PART II

Poems

Time

Songs of Jerusalem and Myself

translated by Harold Schimmel

PART I

Sleep in Jerusalem

While a chosen people
become a nation like all the nations,
building its houses, paving its highways,
breaking open its earth for pipes and water,
we lie inside, in the low house,
late offspring of this old landscape.
The ceiling is vaulted above us with love
and the breath of our mouth
is as it was given us
and as we shall give it back.

Sleep is where there are stones.
In Jerusalem there is sleep. The radio
brings day-tunes from a land
where there is day.
And words that here are bitter,
like last year's almond on a tree,
are sung in a far country, and sweet.

And like a fire
in the hollowed trunk of an olive tree
an eternal heart is burning red
not far from the two sleepers.

Song on Caesarea Beach

I swam far out
beyond the jetty and suddenly stopped moving
like a ship at standstill in deep sea,
the excited passengers not knowing the reason.
It was not from tiredness. The sea was quiet
and my strength was with me. I contemplated the uselessness
of returning. Why should a man return to the shore?
I saw it yellow and gray, not like land
but like a horizon, like the one in the west
that marks with a thin line
the beginning of further distances.
Why return?

Then a beating began inside me
like a muffled engine throbbing in a ship.
This was forgetfulness which began to beat:
an engine far too strong for the needs of my life,
too big for my body, more powerful than all memories
and carrying me far out beyond my death.

God's Hand in the World

1

God's hand in the world
like my mother's
in the guts of the slaughtered hen
on Friday.
What does God see beyond the window
as he puts his hand into the world?
What does my mother see?

2

My pain is already an old man:
it has borne two generations
of pains that resemble it.
My hopes put up white tenements
far from the stress in me.

My girl forgot her love on the sidewalk
like a bicycle. All night out, in the dew.

Children sketch my private history
and the history of Jerusalem
with moon chalk on the road.
God's hand in the world.

Songs to Myself

1

My soul is damaged like the lungs of a diamond cutter.
Beautiful and hard are the days of my life.

My body is like a bank note without cover.
If someone demands gold, I'll have to die.

Already my hands are in their place, my eyes are,
my house is, only I still drift.

I drift.
Beautiful and hard are the days of my life.

2

The world and I have eyes in common:
I look with them into it, it looks into me.

If I weep
the world doesn't care.

But if the world weeps into me
I flood my banks.

3

Like an infant messing itself with food
I want to mess myself with the world's problems.

All over my face, my eyebrows,

my shirt, my trousers, the tablecloth.

The dress of my love, my mother,

the mountains and the sky, all the people,
the feet of angels.

Cradle Song

Sleep, my son, sleep.
The song is not a song
and the cradle's not a cradle.
I'm not at hand,
but the distance will draw us off—
me there and you here. Sleep,

my son, sleep.
In my heart there aren't even
wild flowers like
in the empty lot
after the rains.
But words I have in my mouth,
for your sleep, words.

Sleep, my son, sleep.
The orange peels
will resurrect
and be an orange
from your dreams, my son,
and Trumpledor* will find again
his arm. Sleep.

Sleep, my son, sleep,
free of all your clothes.
In the mosque they take off shoes
in the synagogue wear a hat,
in church remove.
You're free of all that—
sleep, my son, sleep.

*Trumpledor: an almost legendary one-armed hero of the Jewish settlement in Palestine.

I Am Big and Fat

I am big and fat.
Against every ounce of fat
was added an ounce of sadness.

16

I was a great stutterer, but since
I learned to lie, my speech pours out like water.
Only my face stayed heavy,
like syllables impossible to pronounce,
stumble-stones, stammering.

Sometimes by eyes still show flashes
like fire from remote guns
very far inside me. Old battle.

I demand of others
not to forget. Myself, only to forget.

In the end, forgotten.

The Bull Comes Home

The bull comes home from his workday in the ring
after drinking coffee with his fighters
and leaving them a note with his exact address
and the place of the red handkerchief.
(The sword stays stuck in his stiff-necked neck.
And it stays.)
And he's at home now
and sitting on his bed, with his heavy
Jewish eyes. He knows
it hurts the sword too, when it plunges into flesh.
In the next reincarnation he'll be a sword:
the hurt will stay.
("The door
is open. If not, the key is under the mat."

He knows the mercy of evening
and true mercy. In the Bible
he is listed with the clean animals.
He is very kosher, chews his cud,
and even his heart's divided and cleft
like a hoof.
Out through his breast break hairs
dry and gray as from a split mattress.

There Are Many Grapes This Year

There are many grapes this year
but there is no peace in my heart. I eat them
Like a mad bird among scarecrows.

A smell of the last fruit has become
a smell of wine
that no one drinks. Big, black
grapes have turned my mouth
into a woman's insides.
Your lips discovered a ripe fig;
they'll stay that way through winter.
People interpreted bright landscapes
of summer's end, but I was thinking
about my love, which will not suffice
to cover this big land.

It has been a long year, filled
with fruit and the dead.
We wait for rain more than ever.
There are many grapes this year; the last are
yellow like the color of wild wasps
which are their death from within.

18

Resurrection

Afterward they'll get up
all at once, and with a sound of moving chairs
face the narrow exit.

And their clothes are wrinkled
and clods of soil and cigarette ash
are scattered over them
and fingers will uncover in an inside pocket
a theater ticket from a long-gone season.

And their faces still show the crisscross
of God's inclinations.
And their eyes are red from so much sleeplessness
underground.

And immediately—questions:
What time is it?
Where did you put mine?
When? When?

One with an antique upturned face
seems looking— Are there clouds?
Or someone
with a very ancient gesture wipes her eyes
and lifts the heavy hair
at her nape.

Flags

Flags
make the wind.
The wind doesn't
make the wind.

The earth makes
our death.
Not us.

Your face turned west
makes the wandering in me,
not my feet. The roads don't
make the wandering in me,
not Abel's murder,
your face does.

Games

Yes. Drop the words on the table
in a crazy heap
in this Japanese game
of delicate sticks.
Take one
without moving the others.
It moved! It moved!

Or another game: warm,
cold, very cold, a little warmer,
very warm, burning . . . cold.
Afterward, she licks

her lips with a pointed tongue,
then, passing a fingertip lightly over them,
closes like an envelope.

Signs and Testimonies
at Gan Haim Grove

1

Face (woman's)
face, sand face between
rows of dark trees, like tracks
of a heavy wheel that passed.
Imprint of a woman's face.

And an abandoned shoe
filled with sky.
Don't be afraid: no more
will it be filled with a foot.
It won't go.
Just one shoe.

2

Which cloud? The one that was. Was
when? Which one?
A table, a teapot, a cloud, all these
in the past now,
like passing verbs.
A few swimming strokes
remembered from last summer.
(Give regards to whom?
From whom?)

Clouds colored themselves gold
and were beautiful, or bamboo cane
creaked in a dream of a long journey.
A woman undressing in a rickety shack.
The combination—well known.

Evidence

1

It was like silver, like certain.
It hurt.

Smell of the yellow flower calling up desert.
They were three. Face of the one
the face of an eagle. The second was called
to a different place
and went

2

They met among trees.
Cast their love and shadow groundward
and remained standing.
Pointed that way
and said: That way
must be the Dead Sea. That's
where we die.

Behind them were sad animals
one beside the other.

Her thighs were broad and conclusive.
Her head final.

Forehead known.

3

Or evidence of tree on humans:
  Two.
  They sat beneath me,
  they lay down.
  After that I didn't see them.
Deference of the fathers will shield them, or
some other great cloak.

White Negress

Again I long for
strange lighted windows.
Maybe a man, maybe stands, maybe
before a mirror.
Or that white snow falls inside,
a strange king lies
on a woman that might have
been mine.

A white Negress on the Street of the Abyssinians
that has the voice of a daring boy
before it breaks.

When I'll sit with her in a hot bath
I'll hear from the alleys
arguments on religions.

Who Was There?

In these after-night hours:
no longer words,
only longitudes, lines
on a map,
a few numbers.
Not even that.

And here the gate:
I never imagined
loneliness as a gate:
I thought
a wall.

And the call of the guard in me:
Halt!
Who goes there?

Who *was* there?

Suicide Attempts of Jerusalem

Tears, here, don't soften
the eyes. They only polish
the hardness of faces, like rock.

Suicide attempts of Jerusalem:
She tried again on the ninth of Ab.*

She tried in red and in fire
and in slow destruction
by wind and white dust.

She'll never succeed;
but she'll try again and again.

*The anniversary of the destruction of the temple.

My Father, My King

My father, my king, groundless love
and groundless hate have formed my face
like the face of this dry land.
The years have made me a taster of pain.
Like a wine-taster I distinguish
between kinds of silence,
and know what is dead. And who.

My father, my king, may my face
be not torn by laughter or weeping.
My father, my king, make all that happens
between lust and sadness
not torment me too much; make all things
I do against my will
seem by my will. And my will
like flowers.

I've Been Invited to Life

I've been invited to life. But
I see my hosts showing signs
of weariness and impatience.
Trees stir, clouds become
more and more silent, hills shift
from place to place, the sky is yawning.
And in the nights winds move
things uneasily: smoke, people, lights.

I sign the guest book
of God: I was here, I stayed on,
I loved it, it was great, I was guilty, I betrayed.
I was much impressed by the warm welcome
in this world.

Our Love Has Reached Its End

Our love has reached its end.
Time's defense lines are broken,
brave lies fall one by one.

My city, Jerusalem, is a stage
on which I appear from time to time
in a tragic pose.
She remembers similar ones
from Jeremiah
with his "My intestines! My intestines!"—
a crazy bagpipe,
a sensitive land mine of weeping and wailing.

Our love has reached its end.
And soon the old blunt knives
will be out,
for a new encounter of pain and show.

Darwin's Theory

I speak in the name of those
who according to Darwin's theory should have
died and vanished generations ago. I'm
one of them. My genitals swell in a last flowering,
instruments of my fruits and my love. My bones,
which have supported my life and served it faithfully,
turn, slowly, into final implements,
installations of my end.

The weakness which takes hold of my memory
to remember my son and Jerusalem is the same weakness
which is in my knees and my neck.
The same pain. The same peace.

On a Plane

1

I direct the jet
of cool air
to my temple. Afterward
to between my legs.
Like a radiant beam of the early saints.

The plane thinks it is
a passenger plane,
but it is a bomber:
I'm a bomb.

2

I tour the world
in death throes.
Reflexes of fear and hope
move me from country
to country.

Besides great weariness
I have nothing in common with the sea
down there. Wariness
to be what it is,
what I am.

Aunt Amalia Died

Aunt Amalia died in the quiet of her days.
Last of my father's sisters,
his last echo
in this world.

When I, in calm despair, scratch
at the nape of my neck, I feel its hardness.
That comforts me a little.

Her life was never so good
or bad I'd have
to swear by it, falsely.

In the history of my love she has no chapter.
But I'll have to take
her eternity into consideration.

Aunt Amalia died.
Last of my father's seven sisters,
his last face here.

Love in a Season of Truth

What grows,
what thinks
in this spring?

What of the night? You, you of the night—
a signaling of you.

And the voice what? Blood
in the channels of your transparent body
(you hear it).

Washing hands, cutting fingernails.
Yell. Rough combing without water.
Hurts.
("What do you want from me?")

And telling the truth.
Yes, yes, be fruitful and multiply!
Yes, yes.

Just as It Was

Just as it was.
When the water we drank in the nights, afterward,
was all the wine in the world.

And doors, I'll never remember
whether they open in or out,
switches at the entrance to your house
to turn on lights, for ringing or silence.

We wanted it that way. Is that the way we wanted it?
In our three rooms,
by the open window,
you promised me there would be no war.

I gave you a watch instead of
a wedding ring, good and round time,
the ripest fruit
of sleeplessness and forever.

Last Your Hair Dried

Last your hair dried.
When we were already far from the sea,
when words and salt, which mixed on us,
separated from each other
with a sign,
and your body no longer showed
signs of terrible antecedents.
In vain we forgot a few things on the beach,
as a pretext to return.
We did not return.

And these days I remember the days
on which your name was fixed like a name on a ship.
And how we saw, through two open doors,
a man thinking, and how we looked
at the clouds with the ancient look
we inherited from our fathers
waiting for rain,
and how at night, when the world had cooled,
your body held on to its heat a long time
like a sea.

We Did It

We did it in front of the mirror
and in the light. We did it in darkness,
in water and in the high grass.

We did it in honor of man
and in honor of beast and in honor of God.
But they didn't want to know about us,
they'd already seen our sort.

We did it with imagination and colors,
with confusion of reddish hair and brown
and with difficult gladdening
exercises. We did it
like wheels and holy creatures
and with chariot feats of prophets.
We did it six wings
and six legs.

But the heavens
were hard above us
like the earth of the summer beneath.

During Our Love Houses Were Completed

During our love houses were completed
and someone, beginning then,
learned to play the flute. His études
rise and fall. You can hear them
now when we no longer fill each other
as birds fill a tree,
and you change coins, compulsively,
from country to country,
from urge to urge.

And even though we acted madly,
now it seems we didn't swerve much
from the norm, didn't distrub
the world, its people and their sleep.
But now it's over.

Soon
of us two there won't be left either
to forget the other.

You Return

You return, not of your own will,
like the sea by its laws.
The waters of Greece and Cyprus on your lips.
The waters of Brindisi
drying in your hair, at my side,
in this sand
whose last memory is the last wave.

Here death is not
that deep: "You can
stand in it."

Salt in the sky, peace in my heart.
These are days of quiet
and of joined branches on the beach.
Birds descended to the water.
"In this season they get mixed up
sometimes and come to a place
they have not come to."

In Front of the Concrete Wall

In front of the concrete wall
I saw you
lit by the last sun, and beautiful
with first doubts.

On the roof, clothes hung up to dry
were forgotten.
Clothes that had your body's shape.

And like a man who enters
another's words,
other seasons
entered us
and did not let us finish.

Love on a Friday Afternoon

A braided challah, you and me
with sabbath-love.

In the room I blacken your skin
with fresh newspaper fingers.

You hear a tune in your ears
and in them still
the leftover murmuring of my lust,
like in an ashtray.

The sun's too much for you:
you'll put dark glasses
on your eyes.

The world will see you
darker than me.

Navel

In our time there are no longer
declarations of war—
there is war.
And there are no declarations of love.

In a light nightgown
split to the chin, you stood up against me.
One word
(the madwoman laughed in the other room),
one deeply sunk word:
navel.

In the Morning

In the morning I stand near your bed.
My shadow falls on your face
deepens your sleep
adding a little more night.

Like fingers of a smoker
your soul is stained—
addicted to love.

I love you
with all my being, with all my
still being here.

I Sat in Happiness

Your eyes suffered great cold
and great heat
like beautiful glass
and stayed lucid.

I sat in happiness. Like
the straps of a knapsack,
love cut deep into my heart's shoulder.

Your eyes enforced
a new biography.

I sat in happiness. And from now on
I'll be just one side
in the dictionary,
the said or the explained.

Your eyes count and count.

Love Gifts

I gave you, for
your earlobes, for your fingers,
I gilded the time on your wrist,
I hung many shining things on you
so that you'd move in the wind
for me, chime softly over my head,
to soothe my sleep.

I stuffed your bed with apples
(as it is written in the Song of Songs)
so we'd roll smoothly
on a red, apple-bearing bed.

I covered your skin with delicate, pink fabric
transparent as baby lizards
which have eyes of black diamonds in summer nights.

You enabled me to live for a few months
without needing a religion
or a *Weltanschauung.*

You gave me a letter opener of silver:
letters like these aren't opened like that. They're
torn, torn, torn open.

The Last One

The last one
who doesn't run
in a sudden shower
but walks slowly
as before
is first for love,
earmarked
for later.
He'll arrive,
hair
stuck to his forehead
with a smell
of drying wool,
and will love.

Threading

Loving each other
started like that: threading
loneliness into loneliness
with patience
and trembling, exact fingers.

Longing for the past
colored our eyes with a double assurance
of what will never change
and one can never return to.

Yet—one of us
the heart must kill
on one of its skirmishes
(if not you, me)
when it returns empty-handed,
like Cain, a boomerang
from the fields.

Avigayil—Not the Biblical One

Traveled
after the disappointment in love
turned into
a carrier pigeon, light of wing,
and on her right foot the bikini
ring that rolled
to her ankle. (Also
an amulet.)

She stops becoming
and turns into
a superstition,
like a black cat
or a hand with outstretched fingers
or a certan number
or a luminous sky-blue color.

Her desires come out
every hour exactly
like a cuckoo clock.

Try to love her
at exactly twelve o'clock
(in the afternoon or midnight).

Toward the Seventies

A man died whose last name
was like the name of the city
where I was born.
Thus my childhood dies
again and again.

I live now in Jerusalem.
I live, live, live
with quiet stubbornness.

Toward the seventies, decade of blazes.
I gather memories like dry twigs,
thorn and thistle.

Yet I was born in the gay and flaming twenties.
Only once, on a Passover night,
was I sick and very quiet.

My soul—
the folds remained
like in an old letter
I never dared unfold again.

Here.
Yes.
From here
the tearing begins.

My Friend's Father

I saw my friends's father.
Now he no longer speaks aloud
to himself in the street.
A public servant, retired, in twilight.

Compared to him Buber is an eternal student,
arguing on with sweet indulgence.
And Herzl too, leaning on a ship's railing,
his innocent beard streaming in warm dialogue.

"This life is a constant departure
from houses."
The sum of all the stairs
I have already descended
would lift me clear
to heaven.

He Who Relies on Time

He who relies on time
to heal will lose both time and healing.
Time will go by, healing won't come.

He'll set up a draftsman's desk
for his thoughts—
angles and many rulers—
and a weeping lamp bends over him.

Joy and festival will reach
him stammering
like some heavy drink from a dark bottle.

He cannot stay:
the earth already knows too much
about him, even
before he's laid in.

The Death of A. G.

Half an hour ago
my crying stopped.
It's strange and quiet now,
like a factory at evening.

I want to make propaganda
for your death.
I sift your letters
from the others
set apart for life—not so long,

and maybe not better.
I pull the sky down close to my eyes
like someone nearsighted,
to read.

I can't understand your death in London
in the mist,
as I can't understand
my life, here in the bright light.

Bitter Lemon

Bitter lemon, what do you want
from me? I want you to suck me
devour me be bitter with me
and die with me. Sweet mouth,
red mouth's what I want.

Bitter lemon, after that what,
what will we say to them? You're no
honeydew, you're no
honeymoon lodge for my night. You're much, much more.
My mouth will die in you
red, and with my mouth—my rage.

When a Man Changes

When a man changes, he'll always
be a loser—even those not dead
will die—and his belongings will be shifted
from place to place without resurrection.

When a man changes, his son will ask:
"Who slept here last night?"
His tears will flow inside and never dry,
his flesh will wander before the
wandering of his bones, and his sleep
will be scattered in many and far countries.

When a man changes, you can't see his face.
He is like God: he hasn't the
semblance of a body. And those who knew him
will pass through him. He's less than a
mirror, less than a window.

He'll sign letters, unread,
and let his photos develop forever, he'll order
shoes and not take them, and he'll forget
his coat in the wardrobes of strangers.

He'll leave them his dead body
so at least they'll
learn something about him.

Grown Up

They tapped me on the back
as for a child perplexed
in swallowing. They hit me still
and I'm grown up and swallow quietly.
I've learned to read their worthy
penmanship, and also my enemies' script.

Reading music was harder
still, and now I must discern
and read the eyes of those I meet.
And *prove* myself as by Pythagoras'
theorem: I build about me squares and planes
to prove what I really want
and to remain alone in the midst.

My Father's Memorial Day

When the moon is full,
it will be my father's memorial day.
It's always so.

The day of his death will never fall
in summer or in spring.

I put little stones on his tomb:
a sign I was here,
the calling card of one alive
on the big stone of my father. My father,
cause and effect,
your alarm clock breaks my body.

Two sabbath candles of my mother
travel gently side by side in the street,
towed by a ship, not seen.

From a gym hall the hollow echo
of high screams,
vapor and queer sweat
with a smell of girls' thighs and wet rubber.

Father, I now like to wash and comb my hair.
Aside from this, I haven't changed.

The scant information on your tombstone
is less than a passport.

There's no police to tell
I'm a murderer.

When I get home I'll lie down,
arms spread as if crucified.

It calms me,
Father.

Jerusalem 1967

1

This year I traveled far
to view the quiet of my city.
Rocking soothes a baby, distance soothes a city.
I lived in my longing. I played a game
of four severe squares of Yehuda Halevi:
my heart— my self,   the east,   the west.

I heard bells ringing in time's religions,
but the howl I heard within
is still from my Judean Desert.

Now that I'm back, I cry again.
At night the stars come up like bubbles from the drowned.
Each morning I cry the scream of a newborn baby
from the blind chaos of houses and all this great light.

2

Light against the Tower of David, light
on the Church of Maria, light on the Fathers
asleep in their double graves, light on your face
from within, light on the transparent honey
cakes, light on the clock face, and time
is lighted passing between your thighs
when you take off your dress.

Lighted the round cheeks of my childhood,
lighted the stones that wished to be
lighted, with those that wished to
sleep in the darkness of squares.

Lighted the spiders of railings, and
cobwebs of churches and acrobats of
spiral stairs. But of all these, most
is lighted the true and terrible X ray
in letters of white bones and lightning:
Mene   Mene   Tekel   Upharsin.

3

In vain you'll look for barbed-wire fences.
You know such things
don't disappear. Another city, perhaps,
is now cut in two: two lovers
separated; other flesh tormented
by these thorns, refusing to be stone.

46

In vain you'll look. You lift your eyes unto the hills.
Perhaps there? Not these hills, accidents of geology,
but The Hills. You ask
without raising the voice, without question mark,
to do your part in asking questions
gone now. But a great weariness wants you with all your heart
and gets you. Like death.

Jerusalem, the only place in the world
where even the dead have a right to vote.

4

It's not time that takes me from my childhood,
but this city and everything in it. Now
to have to learn Arabic, to reach Jericho
from both sides of time; and length of walls
added to height of towers and domes
vast without limit. All these
widen my life and force me
to migrate anew from the smell
of rivers and forest.

My life's stretched out; thinning like cloth,
transparent. You can see through me.

5

The city plays hide-and-seek between names:
Jerusalem, El-Kuds, Shalem, Jeru, Yeru,
whispering: Y'vus, Y'vus, Y'vus, in darkness.
Weeping with longing: Aelia Capitolina, Aelia, Aelia.
She comes to all who call her
at night, alone. But we know
who comes to whom.

6

Jerusalem stone is the only stone
that hurts. It has a network of nerves.
From time to time Jerusalem gathers
to mass protest like the tower of Babel.
But with big clubs God-The-Police beats
her back: houses razed, walls torn down,
and then once more the city disperses, midst jabbering
prayers complaint and random cries from churches
and synagogues and minaret shout from mosques.
Each one to his place.

7

I and Jerusalem like blind man and cripple.
She sees for me
until the Dead Sea, until the end of days.
And I hoist her on my shoulders
and walk blind in my darkness beneath.

8

On this clear autumn day
I build Jerusalem anew.
Foundation scrolls
fly in the air, birds, thoughts.

God is angry with me
because I force him, always,
to create the world from Beginning:
Chaos, Light, Second Day, to
Man and back again.

9

In the morning the shadow of the Old City falls
on the New. In the afternoon, the reverse.
Nobody profits. The muezzin's prayer
is wasted on the new houses. The ringing

of bells rolls like a ball, and rebounds. Seraphic
praise from synagogues will fade like gray smoke.

At the end of summer I breathe this air,
the parched and aching. A silence
like many shut books is thought:
many closed books, most of whose pages are
stuck like eyelids in the morning.

10

I go up David's Tower,
a little above the most exalted prayer,
halfway to heaven. Some
of the ancients succeeded: Muhammad, Jesus
and others. But didn't find rest in heaven;
they entered a higher excitement. But
the applause for them hasn't let up
below.

11

Jerusalem is built on vaulted foundations
of a held-back shout. Without a reason
for the shout, the foundations would give, the city would
    totter;
if the shout is shouted, Jerusalem would explode skyward.

12

Poets come with evening into the Old City
and leave it loaded with images
and metaphors and little maxims
and twilight similes between vaults and rims.
Darkening fruits
and wrought-iron filigree of the heart.

I lifted my hand to my forehead
to wipe the sweat
and brought up Else Lasker-Schüler

by chance. Light and small as she was in her life,
how much more so in her death. But her poems!

13

Jerusalem port city on the shores of eternity.
The Holy Mount is a huge ship, a luxurious pleasure
liner. From the portholes of her Western Wall happy
saints look out, travelers. Hasidim on the dock wave
good-bye, shout hurrah till we meet again. She's
always arriving, always sailing. And the gates and the docks
and the policemen and the flags and the high masts of
        churches
and mosques and the smokestacks of synagogues and the
        boats
of praise and waves of mountains. The sound of the ram's horn
        is heard: still
another sailed. Day of Atonement sailors in white uniforms
climb among ladders and ropes of seasoned prayers.

And the trade and the gates and the gold domes:
Jerusalem is the Venice of God.

PART II

Spy

Many years ago
I was sent
to spy out the land
beyond the age of thirty.

And I stayed there
and didn't go back to my senders,
so as not to be made
to tell
about this land

and made
to lie.

End of Summer Evening in Motsa

A lone bulldozer fights with his hill
like a poet, like all who work here alone.
A heavy lust of ripe figs
pulls the evening's ceiling to the level of the earth.
Fire has already eaten the thorns
and death won't have to do a thing except
fold up like disappointed flames.
I can be consoled: a great love
can also be a love for landscape.
A deep love for wells, a burning for olive trees,
or digging like bulldozers alone.

My thoughts are always polishing my childhood
till it's become like a hard diamond,
unbreakable, to cut
into the cheap glass of my maturity.

Hike with a Woman

When after hours of walking
you discover suddenly
that the body of the woman stepping beside you
wasn't meant
for travel and war,

and that her thighs have become heavy
and her buttocks move like a tired flock,
you swell with a great joy
for the world
in which women are like that.

The Death of Celan

I heard about it in London.
They said he killed himself.

The same rope
was tugging lightly at my neck.
But it wasn't a rope: he
died by water.
The same water, water, water.

Last metaphor:
a life like a death.
(The same water, water, water.)

Psalm

A song on a day
some building contractor
cheated me. A psalm.
Plaster falls from the ceiling,
the wall is sick, paint cracks like lips.

The vines I've sat under, the fig tree,
all are words. The rustling of leaves
gives an illusion of God and of justice.

I dip my dry look
like bread into the softening death
that is always on the table before me.
Already my life has turned
my life into a revolving door.

I think of those who, in happiness and success,
have left me behind, those
who like pampered and brilliant grapes
are carried for show between two
and those who are also carried
between two and they are wounded or dead. A psalm.

When I was a child I sang in the synagogue choir,
I sang until my voice broke. I sang
first voice and second voice. I'll sing
until my heart breaks, first heart and second heart.
A psalm.

My Portion

Your eyes quiet as mouths.
Your mouth like under the surface of water.
Your face like sand shifting.

Thus you gathered your hair
you gathered the days and the words
in what other times would call
a home

"Never again"—never
is also eternity,
my taste of eternity,
my portion in it.

These Are Preparations for a Journey

These are preparations for a journey. You open
the window. (Don't close it! the air is changing.) A dry
leaf on the bed. I begin to long
for things that are with me, as if they were not.
Preparations for a journey. No eating. No walking.
No standing together. And each night distances
are filled into people like milk
into bottles outside their door. These are preparations
for a journey. My father was trapped inside the holy ark.
The night after Simchat Torah,*, shut with all the glittering
scrolls in the dark. He weeps softly, the way he never
wept in his life. He speaks, muffled, with *his* voice
and my son's. Calls me "my father" and "my son" alternately.
The hammering of his fists from within
stays with me always. These are preparations for a journey.

Man was created to walk upright, on two,
but sometimes his soul wants to stretch out on all four
and lie inside him, only this. Preparations for a journey.

*Feast of the Law.

In a Foreign Country

In a foreign country you must love
a girl who is a history student.
You lie with her in this grass
at the foot of these hills
and between yells and groans
she'll tell you
what happened here in the past.
"Love is a serious matter": I
never saw animals laughing.

Instructions for a Waitress

Don't clear the glasses and plates
from the table. Don't rub
the stain from the cloth: It's good to know
people were here before me.

I buy shoes which were on another man's feet.
(My friend has thoughts of his own.)
My love is another man's wife.
My night is "used" with dreams.
On my window raindrops are painted,
in the margins of my books are notes by others.
On the plan of the house in which I want to live
the architect has drawn strangers near the entrance.
On my bed is a pillow, with
a hollow of a head now gone.

Tourist in Jerusalem

Refreshing girl
like Jericho oranges with leaves
attached so you're convinced
they're fresh.

A girl is such with her dreams
from her green country,
so they'll believe her.

And my love is carved
as
from olive wood. As for tourists.

Night* with an Armenian suffix:
Le-li-an.
Clear like the white in the eye at night
Ai, tallow, tallow.

Lai-la, in Hebrew.

Damascus Gate in Jerusalem

I forget how the road was
a month ago, but I remember it
from the Crusader era, for example.

(Excuse me, this fell. Is it yours?
The stone? Not this, this fell
nine hundred years ago.)

A great gate and at its feet
a little whelp gate.
A blind old man bends to tie
the shoe of his baby grandchild.

(Excuse me, where can I find the Public
Forgetter?)

A childhood grown old is my maturity:
Fever of my days, "shower of all my days," said
Dylan, who is flood tide.

"In the courtyards of our Lord they'll flourish." What are
those courtyards? Like what?

Medlar

I always forget to ask
if it's allowed to eat
the medlar fruit, if it's forbidden.
This name might well have been
a woman's name
of the proudest, that live only once.

I'm a lonely man,
and at the terrible weddings
I've broken more glass than bridegrooms.

My eyes to the waterfall of words
within.
My dark blood—
my true coat.

Poem on the Renovation of My House

With eyes that have seen the gold of Kuwait
and the black cream of oil,
Taleb is at work reconstructing my house
for several thousand pounds
which he changes into dinars; then
to the gold within his eyeballs.

He raises my roof that fell in.
Like an elegant tennis player he flicks plaster
on the walls of my room, and so changes
my biography.

Coiled springs under his feet, he passes
through the Old City after work.
A sweet, meandering and twisting river
in deep and blue charm,
like ribbons in long hair. Taleb
sees a stranger covered with golden down
all over her body: a hairy alien beast
making shadows dance in the alleys. He sees
a policeman riding a white horse,
wings of a parachuted angel on his chest.

Blessed is summer,
the grass on the slope is burnt.
Burning, too, is a language.

With All the Severity of Compassion

Count them.
You may count them. They
are not like the sand on the shore. They
are not like the boundless stars.
They are like lonely people
at the corner, and on the street.

Count them. See them
seeing your heaven through ruined houses.
Come out from the stones and
go back. Where? But count them
because they spur their days with dreams
yet walk free, and their hopes,
which are not tended, are open wounds.
They will die of them.

Count them.
Too early, they learned to read the terrible
writing on the wall. To read and write
on other walls,
while the feast goes on in silence.

Count them. Be present;
they have already used all the blood, and
are still short, as in a dangerous operation,
when one is tired and defeated
like ten thousand. For who judges
and what is judgment
if not with the full meaning of night
and with all the severity of compassion.

Too Many

Too many olive trees in the valley.
Too many stones on the hill's slope.
Too many dead, too little
earth to cover them all.
And I must return to the landscapes painted
on bank notes
and to my father's face on coins.

Too many remembrance days, too little
remembering. My friends have forgotten
what they learned in their youth.
And at a hidden place my love lies
and I am always outside,
food for the hungry winds.

Too much tiredness, too few eyes
to hold it. Too many clocks,
too little time. Too many oaths
on the Bible. Too many roads, too few
ways for a man to really go:
to his destiny.
Too many hopes
that fled their masters.
Too many dreamers. Too few dream
whose solution would change
the history of the world
like Pharaoh's dreams.

My life closes behind me.
And I am outside, a dog
for the cruel and blind wind
pushing always at my back.
I am trained: rise and sit,
waiting to lead him through the streets
that might have been my real life.

Advanced Training for Angels

After the training on round targets
(my life is round like them,
with the black bull's-eye of my childhood
in the center, where I'm vulnerable),
after the training on round targets,
training with dummy men: a head
like a head. A man fleeing.
Or people passing slowly:
a child playing, a man seated in his chair,
my love, at her window,

all passing slowly before the riflemen
on the hill of the broken red
tiles at the edge of the world.

It's Terrible to Identify

It's terrible to identify the dead
after an earthquake, or after a battle.
But it's more terrible to identify them
when they are alive and walking.
Or at seven in the evening
up the street.
When forgetting is gone
but remembrance won't come in its place.

Eternity colors itself with eternity,
water dies in water
and rises from water,
clouds move only among clouds.
Not so with men:
they have to move
among iron and stone,
among all that does not love them.

I had an uncle in whose body
iron from the first World War
remained scattered
till after the second.
When he died, they separated again:
from the iron they made more shells,
from my uncle new uncles,
a new forgetting.

Sort of Apocalypse

The man under his fig tree telephoned the man under his vine:
"Tonight they definitely might come.
Armor-plate the leaves. Secure the tree.
Call the dead home, and make ready!"

The white lamb said to the wolf:
"The human race bleats and my heart aches.
No doubt there'll be close combat there.
At our next meeting we'll discuss it."

All the Nations (united) will stream into Jerusalem
to see if the Law went forth from Zion, and meanwhile

seeing it's now spring
they'll pick flowers,

and beat sword into plowshare and plowshare into sword
then back again, and again and again, without stopping.

Maybe, from so much beating and grinding,
the iron of war will die out.

Half the People in the World

Half the people in the world
love the other half.
Half the people
hate the other.
Must I because of them and of them
go, and wander, and endlessly change
like rain in its cycle, and sleep among rocks, and be rough like
    olive trunks,

and hear the moon bark at me,
and camouflage my love with worries,
and grow like the wavering grass
between the railroad tracks,
and live in the earth like a mole,
and be with roots and not with branches,
and without my cheek on angel's cheek,
and make love in the first cave
and marry my wife under the canopy
of beams which holds up earth,
and play out my death, always
to the last breath and the last
words without understanding,
and set up flagpoles above my house
and a shelter beneath it. And go out
upon the roads made only for return and pass
all the terrible stations—
cat, stick, fire, water, slaughterer,
between the kid and the angel of death?
Half the people love,
half hate.
And where is my place between
the so well-matching halves,
and through what crack will I see the
housing projects of my dreams,
and the barefoot runners on the sands,
or at least the wave
of the girl's handkerchief, by the hill?

All the Generations Before Me

All the generations before me
donated me, bit by bit, so that I'd be
erected all at once
here in Jerusalem, like a house of prayer
or charitable institution.
It binds. My name's
my donors' name.
It binds.

I'm approaching the age
of my father's death. My last
will's patched with many patches.
I have to change my life and death
daily to fulfill all the prophecies
prophesied for me. So they're not lies.
It binds.

I've passed forty.
There are jobs I cannot get
because of this. Were I in Auschwitz
they would not have sent me out to work,
but gassed me straightaway.
It binds.

I Am a Man Alone. I Am Not a Democracy*

I am a man approaching his end.
What seems like youthfulness in me is not
youthfulness, but madness,
because only death can halt this madness.

And what seems like deep roots I put down
is nothing but entanglement on
the surface: spastic knots and cramp of grasping hands,
jumbled ropes and mania of chains.

I am a man alone. I am not a democracy.
The executive, the loving and the legislative power
in one body. The eating, gluttonous, and the vomiting power,
the hating power and power of hurting,
blind power and mute power.
I was not elected. I am a demonstration, I carry
my face like a slogan. It's all written there. Everything.
Please, no need to use tear gas,
I already weep. No need to disperse me,
I am dispersed,
and the dead, too, are a demonstration.
When I visit my father's grave, I see
the tombstones carried high in the hands
of the dust beneath:
they're a mass demonstration.
I think of forgetting as of a slowly ripening fruit,
which once ripe will never be eaten, because it won't be
and won't be remembered:
its ripeness is its forgetting. When I lie
on my back my bones fill
with a sweetness
of my little son's breath.
He breathes the same air as I,
sees the same sights,
yet my breath is bitter and his breath is sweet
like rest in the bones of the tired.
The memory of my childhood be blessed: his childhood.

*This is part of a long autobiographical poem, "The Journey of the Last Benjamin of
Tudela."

66

Jews in the Land of Israel

We forget where we came from. Our Jewish
names from the exile reveal us,
bring up the memory of flower and fruit, medieval cities,
metals, knights that became stone, roses mostly,
spices whose smells dispersed, precious stones, much red,
trades gone from the world.
(The hands, gone too.)

The circumcision does it to us,
as in the Bible story of Shechem and the sons of Jacob,
with pain all our life.

What are we doing here on our return with this pain?
The longings dried up with the swampland,
the desert flowers for us and our children are lovely.
Even fragments of ships, that sunk on the way,
reached this shore,
even winds reached. Not all the sails.

What are we doing
in this dark land that casts
yellow shadows, cutting at the eyes?
(Sometimes, one says even after forty
years or fifty: "The sun is killing me.")
What are we doing with souls of mist, with the names,
with forest eyes, with our lovely children, with swift blood?

Spilled blood isn't roots of trees,
but it's the closest to them
that man has.

A Song of Praise to the Lovely Couple Varda and Schimmel

Jerusalem in the week of the marriage of
Schimmel: I saw a foreign beatnik shoulder
his wrapped guitar like a rifle.
I saw a beggar put out a jingling hand
at the entrance to the public pissoir across from
buttoning men. And in the Russian compound
I heard at night fresh whores
who sang and danced in jail:
Esty, Esty, Esty, take me.

Jerusalem sunk in audiovisual love,
Jerusalem still drunk,
froth of tourists on her lips.

I take her temperature:
thirty-eight degrees in the shade of her armpits,
one hundred degrees of joy
in the mouth of the gold ring.*

But Motza!†
Schimmel is preparing Motza for his marriage.
From the east seven red bulldozers
cut the mountain like a great wedding cake.
Ten yellow cement mixers, thirty workers
with flags and undershirts of phosphorescent orange.
Twenty-one explosions in the afternoon:
Mazel tov!

Schimmel and Varda are already descending slowly
in the parachute of the white synagogue.
Now they're standing silent, wrapped
in the cellophane paper of God's mercy.

*Asshole, in Hebrew.
†Motza is a village situated on a mountain not far from Jerusalem.

68

Love in one clean room,
like a dream of years of good living
compressed in one minute of sleep.
Schimmel and Varda:

two tranquilizer pills
melting slowly
in the mouth of the excited and crumbling world.

Achziv Poems＊

1

Broken by the sea,
my head a broken tin.
Sea water fills it
and drains out.

Broken by the sea.
A dirge my lament,
froth on the lips of the cliffs.
The sea has rabies,
has sea sickness,
more dog than dog,
more sea than all seas.

Broken by the sea
my lament.

＊Achziv: an old village on the north coast of Israel.

2

Old millstones separated
and laid out for show
at the two ends of the village.
From great longing
they continue to grind between them
lovers' time.

Naked people in the sand talk about
political problems. It's absurd!
Little piles of clothes in the distance.
Birds cry from an island. Pink buttocks
and muscles like sleeping fish. It's
absurd even to ask "What's the time?"
when you're naked. A white stripe on your wrist.
Better, dialogue:
"Di-," she said. "alogue," he said.
Di-, di-, di-, alogue, alogue.

Our friend hid his typewriter
in the broom bush. Camouflaged in the branches.
Tak, tak, di-, di-, di-, alogue.

3

All night you lay awake on your back.
There was another wind
and there was a wind like you.
The light of the moon
threw on the wall
one more lattice.
"The key's under the stone near the gate."
In the morning the outline of your body appeared
marked by cigarette butts
on the floor.

4

Your green eyes were
blue for my brown eyes
after this night.

And wrinkles appeared on the sheets:
no, not from age.

5

Around the dead word "we-loved"
covered over by seaweed in the sand
the curious mob crowded.
And until evening we heard the testimonies
of waves, one by one,
how it happened.

6

Much waves, much eyes,
much affliction, much salt,
much sleep, much deceit,
much sadness, song in the nights, much
shells, much sand, the profane, everything.

The explanation—to go on living.
What is our life: so many centimeters of
distraction and tenderness, meat
between the hard skeleton inside
and the hard air outside.

7

My friend saw horses bathing
in the sea at Akko. He saw them and I feel
them galloping. What did we look for
in the sand that Tuesday and Wednesday,
what did we look for?
With a little breath I put out your right ear.

With a little breath I put out your left ear.
With little breaths on both your ears
I lit your lusts. A great
invasion began within us. Our writhing and
twining bodies were witnesses to the greatness of
the tussle.
In vain.

8

Tie your weeping with a chain
and be inside with me.

In the partly ruined house
the light lives by himself.
From the darkness they make delicate silverware
for the last meal.

My fish mouth mouth
and your fish mouth nipple
are attached at night.

After that was a moonlit night
whiter than Atonement Day.
Your weeping burst the chain.
Fled.

9

In the sand we were two-headed Cerberus
with bared teeth. In the afternoon
your one leg was in the east and your second in the west
and I in the middle, leaning on my forelegs,
looking to the sides with suspicion, roaring awfully,
lest they take my prey from me.

Who are you?
A poor Jewish kid from the diaspora,
skullcap on the head. From there. From that time.

72

All night we're together. No
heavy memories, sticky feelings. Just
muscles, tensing and relaxing.

In another continent of time,
the dead rabbis of my childhood appear,
holding the gravestones high over
their heads.
Bound up in the knot of my life.

My God, my God,
Why have you not forsaken me!?

10

With the daring glance of Columbus
I look out between towels hung
in the window. The sun sets
in a red dress.
Four boats pass from evening
to evening from behind a handkerchief.
Salt in the little salt cellar on the table,
and outside all the salt in the world.

Seven crumpled panties
around your bed, for the seven
days we were here.
Seven withered roses
in seven colors.

11

A one-piece bathing suit:
the big voice of the mob.
A crazy somersault.
The applause of my hand on your body,
wild applause.

The dry element and the
moist in a great longing
destroy each other.

Hesitating veins.
Blue trying to look pink.
I live by your ankles.
My member stands up with solemn ceremony
as if to listen.

I'll leave you beside the sea
until your reddish hair goes green,
until my black briefcase is buried in weeds
like a long-sunk ship.
I'll whip cries out of you,
to make up for all the silences.
Heady revenge.
God.

12

I learned
to relate to your cunt
as to a face.

I speak its former language.
Wrinkled, and made of substance older
than all remembered ages, written on a book.

It relates to us
as distant offspring,
playing.

13

Ach seed, ach streaming semen,
Achziv gold oozes
so, so.

Soon the deserted village
will be a second time deserted
by us. Ach you,
hair brown, skin white,
eyes green; but here,
in Achziv, all the red breaks out
in you: you're one
of thirty-six lurking holy incarnadines.
Moss between your thighs,
redskin,
Esau-
ite.

14

Wind, what a waste of wind
you are. To move sand to sand,
me to you, smell to smell.
Wind, what a waste!

Clouds, what a waste of cloud,
not raining, just shifting
the colors of western Galilee a little
for us.

My life, what a waste of life
you are. Just for these days. Here.

15

Tyrus ladders,* lust ladders,
ladders to the roof of Eli's house. Girls
come down, go up, bearing ropes and mattresses,
long hair and underwear to dry. Washday
cries. Laughing-damp won't dry.
Girls go up, come down the ladder.

*Tyrus Ladder—*Sulam Tzur*—the name of the coast in northern
Israel below the Lebanese border, on which Achziv is located.

We see her soul:
it's black and made of fine embroidered net.
We see her pink subconscious,
with dainty lace on it. We see it,
oh, we see it, we see it.

16

In the abandoned house
live a dwarf tamarisk, mint
and sage. Let's visit them
in the afternoon. We'll sit awhile,
rustle with them and send up scents.

There's a red line on your waist
in memory of the elastic.
It will vanish like a sand ledge with the wave,
then we'll know:
our time is ripe to be here.

17

A last night near the window,
outside and in. Hours pass, seven,
nine, ten.   Eleventh hour:
moonlight
turned our bodies into surgical instruments
hard and gleaming with evil.

Another hour, hours, one, two, three,
five: in the first light of dawn
your body was seen caught in the network
of its nerves, like a sheet
that fell during the night and held,
stuck in the branches of the dead tree
before the window.

18

What's it like to be a woman?
What's it like to feel
vacancy between legs and curiosity
under the skirt, in summer, in wind,
and chutzpa* at the haunches?

A male has to live with that odd sack
between his legs. "Where would you like
me to put it?" asked the tailor,
measuring my pants,
and didn't smile.

What's it like to have a whole voice,
that never broke?
To dress and undress   slitherly
slinkily   caressively
like wearing olive oil,
to anoint the body with lithe fabrics,
a silky something,
a murmuring nothing of peach or mauve?
A male dresses with crude gestures of
buckling and edgy undoing,
angles, bones and stabs in the air,
and the wind's entangled in his eyebrows.

What's it like to "feel a woman"?
And your body dreams you.
What's it like to love me?

Leavings of a woman on my body,
and signs of the male on yours
augur the hell
which awaits us
and our mutual death.

*Chutzpa: unmitigated effrontery or impudence. [Yiddish]
    —*The Random House Dictionary of the English Language*

77

19

If longings start—longings
to be among these houses near this sea,
we'll already be far from them.

My heart's keeners began
too soon, while I'm still here,
to lament and pluck at my blood and at the sea's sand
and weeds; to beat with fists on cliff,
on sand and on your breasts.

The sea retreats from my face.
My face is the floor of the sea: dry
with cracks and rocks and savage winds.
I grew up like that,
the memories of the soft green sea still on my face.

20

After these days, I still don't know much
about you. The palm remains bent to the east
even with no wind from the west. A white boat
passes parallel to the coast, hard
and clear like God's fingers. The last will
I write in Achziv, in the sand,
is different from the one I wrote in Jerusalem.
Children's voices buried beneath layers
on the hill reach us in this century
at this hour of the afternoon. They haven't
stopped playing.

The white, licked beam will never return
and be in a ship, the milled gravel
can never become a rock. It tears at
my heart, as it tore at the prophets'; with a sharp
tearing pain a man's turned into a prophet.

It's a good landscape for forgetting and prophecy.
From now on we'll look for windows with other
views. We'll wander from window to window,
from arch to arch.

Soon the abandoned ship's anchor will be
decoration for houses and yards. Our hearts too
will be just an amulet,
hung inside in dreams and blood.

The Buenos Aires Poems

1

All the while
I didn't see the sea. Then
once, at night, you told me about it.
I didn't want to hear, so that
Buenos Aires would be
like Jerusalem without a sea.

Dolores they called you,
Susanna
is the name of your friend, "Chica,"
a driver, passing, called out.

We both were lost
by two who never knew each other:

two losses crying
and laughing together in the dark.

2

Deep passageways, galleries, a display window
with serious playthings, like a brown race horse,
an ivory chess set on
a scarlet flame of velvet,
grave and bitter playing cards like bitter
chocolate, tobacco that contracts the lips with dim
gold. A hard pipe,
pale dice that didn't melt,
remoteness of a bullfight, smell of tanned leather.
A sign implores with quiet weeping:
Do not smoke.
Inflammation of street lamps like of the eyes,
a light that once really hurt.

You die, you cross the river of memory
to eternal memory. Deep passageways.

3

Precise instruments,
very precise instruments.

A woman surprised by mild pain,
something had fled from the face inward,
a shadow laugh.

Her father's fathers
wiped out the Indian peoples.
A guilt of birds
that hurt the air in their flight
remained within her.

Precise instruments,
very precise instruments.

4

Born near the sea in a city *del Mar,*
was loved in a small room far from it,
lived on a street named for a man dead and forgotten.
Even the taxi driver didn't know how to find
the old house with the quiet door.
Wore a striped dress and spun between the stripes
in a whirlpool. Lost
also among large and printed flowers.

I kissed her mouth which a foreign language
had shaped. And so I learned.
"Hello, hello," despairing in my language,
"Ola?" amused and sad in hers.

And in my winter is her summer and in my day her night.
And in my country days get longer and in hers shorter
and her eyes are a process for melting gold in brown
and her body's shape is like the shape of the opening
in my life.

5

Remnants of an Argentinian funeral
cross my path. Three, four,
already without flowers. The grave is far,
a very elegant funeral, thoroughly urban,
with made-up eye, clean-shaven cheek
and a black dress close to the thigh,
in the flight from death.

And there is a man who has nothing
to bring to burial
but the memory of one night.

6

In the hotel. I need two
pillows: one under my head
to prevent memories and one over my eyes
so as not to see what's coming.

In the morning I get out of the bed, in which,
next week, I'll forget my pajamas.
I lather soap on my face
with a brush
made from a single plait of your hair.

Downstairs they set Easter pastries
before me, a whole egg baked
into a sweet cake:
my eyes, too, still closed in sleep.

7

Words hung in the mouth
like a cigarette that didn't light,
and now a migration of birds
begins in me,
from my cold heart to my warm heart.

These birds don't know
I'm the same man (those
outside know it's the same world).

"In this room
two can be strangers
to each other, as in a huge time."

8

A girl on Avenida Santa Fe. Additional
eyes are drawn on hers, lips
smeared with the white of the beautiful dead,
very long eyelashes, her eye's teeth.

A psychology student: fourth
year of the passing leisure
of knowledge in her convex and pleasant brain.

A small gold cross on her neck
(I come from a country where it's real and heavy)
and both of us are at different stages
in the process of giving in;
despair of "the good" is quiet here.
In my country it gushes blood.

"Far off," she said.
The streets begin far off,
are caught in the city and move again
to sea, to plains, to air.

"Anasco." She said the name of her street,
sang it like a question. Also told
her name, like a gravestone with lovely flowers,
a veto against our stay together.

9

Sitting in a dark café
on Coronel Diaz Street.
Bitter hero, dead.

A small cup of coffee was enough
for an extended stay.
A newspaper in a language I didn't know.

I scattered cake crumbs on a plate
as for a bird: you came
eyeing about.

I sit, quiet, see you,
you eat quickly,
fly.

10

We lay
exposed and alike
like two halves of an orange
until the evening
became darker than your voice.

Water can be cried out,
stones not: therefore I return to Jerusalem.
"I'll *miss* you!"
Who taught you
to say a vulgar word like that?

11

Intersection.
Corner of Santa Fe
and Cajau, afternoon, waiting:

Which one of all the shadows is mine?
That's why I raised a hand.
That's why I loved you.

Intersecting streets,
a true cross.

12

Silvia's very much changed: her face
grew longer, but in her eyes black
coal remained, glowing in hope of fire.

I sat with her in a café
called "The Family."
She's proud like young soldiers
after their first battle.

She went through many sorrows,
like those an entire nation goes through
in an extended history
(battles and losses, also victories),
alongside her handsome husband. She still
loves him. He loves her very much.

13

A language sickness.
Swaying drunkenness
in the Chinese restaurant where
they translate from Spanish to Hebrew to English,
and far away from them
to Chinese in red kitchen fires.

How many words are shed on the way
how much blood spilled
how much laughter
how much remains nothing!

14

Closeness to Cordoba: I saw
a Jewish girl
from Poland, from Cordoba in Argentina.

Through her eyes
I go back
to Cordoba in Spain
a long way.

Echoes of eyelids anointed white,
chill and damp tunnels
of pupils
and shadows of long eyelashes
like endless fences.

15

Early in the morning the sun
is taken out from cushions of dark velvet.
Family asset, from generation to generation (ah!),
old candelabrum, gold samovar,
survivors of pillage, rape,
Cossacks, Indians, Missionaries,
Crusaders, Mamelukes
(ah!)

Quickly, get up quickly!
Cologne water with hurried daubing
to the armpits, to the nape,
to between the legs still dreaming.
Quickly, quickly, get outside (ah!).

16

And not for the sake of remembering
you live, but to complete this work
which is yours (nonetheless yours) to complete,
and not for the sake of staying you love
and not for the sake of loving you hurt.

Rash, you are, and rush into tiredness,
impatient like a flight-day from country to country,
bartering good hours of life with blessed
rains, at unknown exchange,
passing to lover to passer-by on Corrientes
Street, the streaming, the streaming.

Vamos, let's go. In other
languages it hurts less. Let's go!
There is an illusion of together
at first; afterward, apart.

17

Mourning ever alert
to what softly happens: light
in the covered mirror, voices
behind the heavy curtain.

Mourning ever alert,
joy loses things, careless.
Things fall from you, unnoticed.
But mourning ever alert.

18

Of this time, with light
through the slats of the blind, a head like
Nefertiti, eyes like Sigmund
Freud—frightened—and a wagon wheel
for a lamp, hanging from the ceiling.
"Like fingernails, I'll trim
this love," and a careful placing
of things on the table: the cup, the book,
the spoon, the salt cellar. All those like a heart
beating slowly. "You're using
me!" (another gloss on love).
"You're thinking along very exact
formulas of a heart broken to well-
defined pieces, like once
a heart broke of love."

19

In the Botanical Garden among names, names,
childhood memory, always look for
a public lavatory or a stand for sticky
sweets. Not to remember names,
to flee, to buy food items
for the last meal.

The shopgirl was frightened by our rush. The wrapping
tore, was changed, tore again.
Paper, boxes, cheese
and fruit rolling knew
of all the helplessness of
keeping together.
"You'll be caught forever
in the rigid grid lines of your city."

20

In this city the sky is always
like a layer of gray plaster;
our lives are healing.
The fracture will close, perhaps.

You may go now. "Go,
go," say the traffic lights. Go,
go in peace.
We deserted each other, we gave it up
so that good people could practice
their goodness on us and not forget their mercy.
Buenos Aires will be a different
city when you're gone. "A city without you," she said,
and went her way.

21

City of Borges and Tzivia,
city of an obelisk that never saw
Egypt, city of Susanna
who had not heard of me,
a space between crying and laughter
without crying and without laughter.

There are houses I
want to live in forever,
as in the Middle Ages
the soul asked to live
in a beautiful and pure body.

City of Eduardo:
I wrote his address down in my notebook,
he also wrote mine down in his.
Most likely we won't meet again.

22

Missa Susanna,
wrath of love and fury of longing.
You set my dreams upon me,
I'll set my voice upon you.
Your thighs red in the fire
and the folds of your dress, dark
in order to recite Kaddish.
Peace upon my soul, peace upon your soul,
amen.

Missa Susanna.
this skinny angel
will not guard me from all evil.
But he makes me feel good
with his big eyes that stay
in place.

Missa Susanna,
the paper is tearing on all sides.
The boy who sold the morning news—
by noon his voice already broke.
Loss of names and their bearers.
My coat is marked inside
and my watch strangles my wrist.

Missa Susanna,
may the clods of the words be sweet
to your lovely mouth. Rest now in peace
on your couch. Remember me,
who was little or much,
remember me in the dim corridors

and the delights that awoke
in the great light.
From sieve to sieve
we fall and diminish

from what place to what place,
amen.

23

Good people that took
me from the plane on a hot night
brought me back to it
after several days, as my blood prepared
to become fuel again for the flight. Same
people, on the same hot night.
But I wasn't the same.

The plane, that sucked burning air
into its engines,
swallowed your love and used it too.

Stopover in Rio,
rent-heart de Janeiro.
Repairable.

24

There's a smell of fresh paint here.
Do not forget, there,
in the closed half of the partly
closed eye, painted
white and forgetting.

A slow count backward
into the darkness dimly lit
with what was.

The room. How lonely and abandoned the Spanish
language was in the room.
Afterward the Hebrew too.

The city that gave me calm
and took it from me.

Ballad in the Streets of Buenos Aires

And a man waits in the streets and meets a woman
Precise and beautiful as the clock inside her room
And sad and white as the wall that holds it

And she does not show him her teeth
And she does not show him her belly
But she shows him her time, precise and beautiful

And she lives on the ground floor next to the pipes
And the water which goes up starts at her wall
And he has decided on softness

And she knows the reasons for the weeping
And she knows the reasons for the holding back
And he begins, and he begins to be like her

And his hair grows long and soft like hers
And the hard words of his country melt in her mouth
And his eyes in tears will look like hers

And the traffic lights light up her face
And she is standing there in the allowed and the forbidden
And he has decided on softness

And they walk in the streets which will be in his dreams
And the rain weeps into them as into a pillow
And restless time has made them into prophets

And he will lose her in the Red light
And he will lose her in the Green and in the Yellow
And the light is always there to serve all loss

And he won't be when soap and lotion run out
And won't be when the clock is set again
And won't be when the dress is raveled out in threads

And she will shut his wild letters in a quiet drawer
And lie down to sleep beside the water in the wall
And she will know the reasons for weeping and for holding back
And he has decided on softness.

Poems

translated by Ted Hughes and Assia Gutmann

King Saul and I

1

They gave him a finger, but he took the whole hand.
They gave me the whole hand; I didn't even take the little finger.
While my heart
weight-lifted its first feelings
he rehearsed the tearing of oxen.

My pulsebeats were like
drips from a tap,
his pulsebeats
pounded like hammers on a new building.

He was my big brother,
I got his used clothes.

2

His head, like a compass, will always bring him
to the sure north of his future.

His heart is set, like an alarm clock,
for the hour of his reign.
When everyone's asleep, he will cry out
until all the stone quarries are hoarse.
Nobody will stop him!

Only the asses bare their yellow teeth
at the end of the road.

3

Dead prophets turned time wheels
when he went out searching for asses
which I, now, have found.
But I don't know how to handle them.
They kick me.

I was raised with the straw,
I fell with heavy seeds.

But he breathed the winds of his histories.
He was anointed with the royal oil
as with wrestlers' grease.
He battled with olive trees,
forcing them to kneel.

Roots bulged on the earth's forehead
With the strain.
The prophets escaped from the arena;
Only God remained, counting:
Seven . . . eight . . . nine . . . ten . . .
The people, from his shoulders downward, rejoiced.
Not a man stood up.
He had won.

4

I am tired,
my bed is my kingdom.

My sleep is just,
my dream is my verdict.

I hung my clothes on a chair
for tomorrow.

He hung his kingdom
in a frame of golden wrath
on the sky's wall.

My arms are short, like string too short
to tie a parcel.

His arms are like chains in a harbor
to carry cargo across time.

He is a dead king.
I am a tired man.

Ibn Gabirol

Sometimes pus
sometimes a poem.

Something always bursts out.
And always pain.

My father was a tree in a forest of fathers
covered in green cotton wool.

Oh, widows of the flesh, orphans of the blood,
I must escape.

Eyes sharp as can openers
Opened heavy secrets.

But through the wound on my chest
God peers into the world.

I am the door
to his apartment.

The Place Where I Have Not Been

The place where I have not been
I never shall be.
The place where I have been
is as though I have never been there. People stray
far from the places where they were born
and far from the words which were spoken
as if by their mouths
and still wide of the promise
which they were promised.

And they eat standing and die sitting
and lying down they remember.
And what I shall never in the world return to
And look at, I am to love forever.
Only a stranger will return to my place. But I will set down
all these things once more, as Moses did,

after he smashed the first tablets.

Out of Three or Four in a Room

Out of three or four in a room
one is always standing at the window.
Forced to see the injustice among the thorns,
the fires on the hill.

And people who left whole
are brought home in the evening, like small change.

Out of three or four in a room
one is always standing at the window.
Hair dark above his thoughts.
Behind him, the voices.
And in front of him the words, wandering, without luggage.
Hearts without provision, prophecies without water
and big stones put there
and staying closed, like letters
with no addresses, and no one to receive them.

If With a Bitter Mouth

If with a bitter mouth you will speak
sweet words, the world will
neither sweeten nor become bitterer.

And it is written in the book that we shall not fear.
And it is also written, that we also shall change,
like the words,
in future and in past,
in the plural or in isolation.

And soon in the coming nights
we shall appear, like strolling players,
each in the other's dream.

And into these dreams
there shall also come strangers
we did not know together.

In My Time, in Your Place

We were together in my time, in your place.
You gave the place and I the time.
Quietly your body waited for the seasons to change.
Fashions passed over it, to shorten, to lengthen,
with flowers or in white silk, clinging.

We swapped human values for those of beasts,
calm and tigerlike and forever.
And for all that, ready to burn any moment
with the dry grass of the end of summer.

I divided the days with you, nights.
We exchanged a look with rain,
I was your Lent and your Mardi Gras
in one body. We were not like dreamers,
even in our dreams.

And in the unquiet, nestled the quiet,
in my time, in your place.

The many dreams I now dream of you
prophesy your end with me—

as the multiplying crowds of seagulls
come where the sea ends.

In My Worst Dreams

In my worst dreams
you, with bright eyes,
are always standing near walls
whose foundation stone
is a heart.

Of all the things I do,
parting is the inevitable one.

In my dreams I always hear a voice—
it is not my voice
and not yours,
neither is it the daughter of your voice.

Eyes creased, my eyes are
like the eyes of exhausted beasts
lusting for days
that have passed with the nights.

They have taken a love mask off me
just as they take a death mask.
They took it without my noticing
as I lay beside you.

It is my true face.

Farewell, You

Farewell, you; your Face, already the Face of memory,
wandering, rising from the world of the dead, and flying, flying.
Face of beasts, Face of water, Face of going
and a forest of whispers,
face of the womb, Face of child.

No longer ours the hours of touch,
no longer ours to say: Now. Now.
Yours was the name of winds, once the wife
of directions, purpose, mirror, and autumn.

Whatever we failed to understand, we sang together.
Generations and the dark, Face of alternation.
No longer mine, unsolved,
locked nipples, buckles, mouths, screws.

Farewell then, you, the never sleeping,
all was fulfilled by our word; that all is of sand.
From now on
dream through your own dreams, the world and all.

Go in peace, go, bundles and cases of death.
Threads, feathers, the household mash, pawn of hair,
whatever will not be, no hand writes,
whatever was not of the body will leave no memory.

A Pity. We Were Such a Good Invention

They amputated
your thighs off my hips.
As far as I'm concerned
they are all surgeons. All of them.

They dismantled us
each from the other.
As far as I'm concerned
they are all engineers. All of them.

A pity. We were such a good
and loving invention.
An airplane made from a man and wife.
Wings and everything.
We hovered a little above the earth.

We even flew a little.

It Was Summer, or the End of Summer

It was summer, or the end of summer,
and I heard then your footsteps, as you went from east to west
for the last time. And in the world
handkerchiefs were lost, and books, and people.

It was summer, or the end of summer,
there were hours in the afternoon,
you were;
and you wore your shroud
for the first time.
And you never noticed
because it was embroidered with flowers.

Two Songs on Caesarea Beach

1

The sea preserves in salt.
Jerusalem preserves in dryness.
And where shall we go?
Now, in the exacting twilight,
to choose.
Not what we shall do
or how we shall live
but to choose the life
whose dreams
will hurt least
in all the nights to come.

2

"Come again next summer"
or words like that
hold my life,
take away my days,
like a line of soldiers
passing over a bridge
marked for exploding.
"Come again next summer."

Who hasn't heard these words?

But who comes again?

Like Our Bodies' Imprint

Like our bodies' imprint,
not a sign will remain that we were in this place.
The world closes behind us,
the sand straightens itself.

Dates are already in view
in which you no longer exist,
already a wind blows clouds
which will not rain on us both.

And your name is already on the passenger lists of ships
and in the registers of hotels
whose names alone
deaden the heart.

The three languages I know,
all the colors in which I see and dream:

None will help me.

God Has Pity on Kindergarten Children

God has pity on children in kindergartens,
He pities school children—less.
But adults he pities not at all.

He abandons them,
and sometimes they have to crawl on all fours
in the roasting sand
to reach the dressing station,
and they are streaming with blood.

106

But perhaps
He will have pity on those who love truly
and take care of them
and shade them,
like a tree over the sleeper on the public bench.

Perhaps even we will spend on them
our last pennies of kindness
inherited from mother,

so that their own happiness will protect us
now and on other days.

Two Quatrains

1

Once I escaped, but I do not remember why or from which God,
I shall therefore travel through my life, like Jonah in his dark fish,
we've settled it between us, I and the fish, we're both in the world's
    bowels,
I shall not come out, he will not digest me.

2

The last rains came on a warm night, in the morning my disaster
    blossomed.
The race is over. Who is first, who second?
After our death we could play: I shall be you, you—me,
in the dead moon, in the returning ancient time, in my window's
tree.

Eye Examination

Go back a bit. Close your left eye.
Still?
Go back a bit further. The wall has moved on.
What do you see?
What do you recognize in the dimness?
I remember a lovely song which went . . .
Now? What do you see now?
Still?—All the time.
Don't leave me. Please. Please.
You're not leaving.
I'm not.
Close one eye. Speak in a loud voice.
I can't hear—I'm already far away.
What do you recognize? What do you see?

Close one sad eye.
Yes.
Close the other sad eye. Yes.
I can see now.

And nothing else.

In the Middle of This Century

In the middle of this century we turned to each other
with half faces and full eyes
like an ancient Egyptian picture
and for a short while.

I stroked your hair
in the opposite direction to your journey.
We called to each other,
like calling out the names of towns
where nobody stops
along the route.

Lovely is the world rising early to evil,
lovely is the world falling asleep to sin and pity,
in the mingling of ourselves, you and I,
lovely is the world.

The earth drinks men and their loves
like wine,
to forget.
It can't.
And like the contours of the Judean hills,
we shall never find peace.

In the middle of this century we turned to each other,
I saw your body, throwing shade, waiting for me,
the leather straps for a long journey
already tightening across my chest.
I spoke in praise of your mortal hips,
you spoke in praise of my passing face.

I stroked your hair in the direction of your journey,
I touched your flesh, prophet of your end,
I touched your hand, which has never slept,
I touched your mouth, which may yet sing.

Dust from the desert covered the table
at which we did not eat.
But with my finger I wrote on it
the letters of your name.

Poem in an Orange Grove

I am abandoned by God. "You're abandoned by God,"
said my father.
God forgot me—
so did he, later.

The scent of orange groves in blossom
was in me for a while. You. Hands sticky
with juice and love. You cried a great cry
and threw two of your last thighs into battle.
and then silence.
You, whose handsome head learned history,
know that only what's past is silent.
Even battles,
even the scent of orange groves.
Blossoms and fruit were on one and the same tree,
above us, in that double season.

Even then we spoke with that foreign
and strange accent of those who will die.

I Was the Moon

My child is very sad.

Whatever I teach him—
geography of love,
strange languages which can't be heard
because of the distance—
my child rocks his little bed towards me in the night.
What am I?

More than forgetting.
The very language of forgotten.
And until he understands what I did
I am as good as dead.

What are you doing with our quiet child?
You cover him with a blanket
like heaven, layers of clouds—
I could be the moon.

What are you doing with your sad fingers?
You dress them with gloves
and go out.

I was the moon.

As for the World

As for the world,
I am always like one of Socrates' disciples,
walking by his side,
hearing his opinions and histories;
it remains for me to say:
yes. Yes, it is like that.
You are right again,
indeed your words are true.

As for my life,
I am always like Venice:
whatever is mere streets in others
within me is a dark streaming love.

As for the cry, as for the silence,
I am always a shofar:

all year long hoarding its one blast
for the Terrible Days.

As for action,
I am always like Cain:
nomad
in the face of the act, which I will not do,
or, having done,
will make it irredeemable.

As for the palm of your hand,
as for the signals of my heart
and the plans of my flesh,
as for the writing on the wall,
I am always ignorant;
I can neither read nor write
and my head is like the
heads of those senseless weeds,

knowing only the rustle and drift
of the wind
when a fate passes through me
to some other place.

She Knows

I know that she knows.
They think she doesn't, but know otherwise.
She knows.

My heart tears with this game
and in the night its blood hears the cry
like the cry of paper tearing
across the forty-two years of my life.

Under a broad vine,
in the yard of a house
in the Valley of Hinnom,
an old woman once told me:
"Because he was burned inside,
his head turned white as snow."
I forget what she was talking about
or whom—
my life is forty-two years of torn paper.

Tourist

She showed me her swaying hair
in the four winds of her coming.
I showed her some of my folding ways of life
and the trick, and the lock.
She asked after my street and my house
and I laughed loudly.
She showed me this long night
and the interior of her thirty years.
I showed her the place where I once laid tefillin.

I brought her chapters and verses
and sand from Eilat
and the handing of the Torah
and the manna of my death
and all the miracles that have not yet healed in me.

She showed me the stages of joy
and my childhood's double.
I revealed to her that King David is not buried in his tomb
and that I don't live in my life.

While I was reflecting and she was eating,
the city map lay open on the table—
her hand on Qatamon,
my hand on hers—
the cup covered the Old City,
ash dropped on the King David Hotel,
And an ancient weeping
allowed us to lie together.

God's Fate

God's fate
is now
the fate of trees rocks sun and moon,
the ones they stopped worshipping
when they began to believe in God.

But he's forced to remain with us
as are the trees, as are the rocks
sun moon and stars.

My Mother Once Told Me

My mother once told me
not to sleep with flowers in the room.
Since then I have not slept with flowers.
I sleep alone, without them.

There were many flowers.
But I've never had enough time.
And persons I love are already pushing themselves
away from my life, like boats
away from the shore.

My mother said
not to sleep with flowers.
You won't sleep.
You won't sleep, mother of my childhood.

The bannister I clung to
when they dragged me off to school
is long since burned.
But my hands, clinging,
remain
clinging.

My Parents' Migration

And my parents' migration has not yet calmed in me.
My blood goes on shaking at its walls,
as the bowl after it is set down.
And my parents' migration has not yet calmed in me.
Winds continually over stones.
Earth forgets the footsteps of those who walk.
An awful fate. Stumps of talk after midnight.
An achievement, a retreat. Night reminds
and day forgets.
My eyes, which have looked a long time into a vast desert,
are a little calmed. One woman. The rules of a game
nobody had ever completely explained. The laws of pain and weight.

115

Even now my heart
makes only a bare living
with its daily love.
My parents in their migration.
On the crossroads where I am forever orphaned,
too young to die, too old to play.
The weariness of the miner
the emptiness of the quarry
in one body.
Archaeology of the future,
museums of what is still to happen.
And my parents' migration has not yet calmed in me.
And from bitter peoples I learned bitter languages
for my silence among the houses
which are always
like ships.

Already my veins, my tendons
are a tangle of ropes I will never undo.
Finally, my own death
and an end to my parents' migration.

To Summon Witnesses

When did I last weep?
The time has come to summon witnesses.
Of those who last saw me weep
some are dead.

I wash my eyes with a lot of water
so as to see the world once more
through the wet and the hurt.

I must find witnesses.

Lately, I have felt for the first time
needle stabs in my heart.
I am not frightened,
I am almost proud, like a boy
who discovers the first hairs in his armpits
and between his legs.

The End of Elul*

I'm tired of summer.
The smoke rising from the convent of the silent nuns
is all I have to say.
This year winter will come late
when we're ready for its coming,
and we won't be.

I'm tired. And curse the three Great Religions,
which won't let me sleep at night
what with bells and howls of muezzins and loud shofars and noisy
     atonements.
Oh, God, close your houses, let the world rest.
Why hast thou *not* forsaken me?
This year the year hesitates.
The summer drags on.
If it weren't for the tears that I have kept back all these years,
I'd have dried up like thorns.

Elul is the last month of summer.

Great battles are conducted within me in dreadful quiet,
with only the sighs of thousands of sweating, naked wrestlers.
There is no iron, and no stone, only flesh, like snakes;
and afterwards, they'll fall away one from the other with surfeit and
    weakness,
and there will be clouds, and there will be rain
when we're ready for it, and we won't be.

Quick and Bitter

The end was quick and bitter.
Slow and sweet was the time between us,
slow and sweet were the nights
when my hands did not touch one another in despair
but with the love of your body
which came between them.

And when I entered into you
it seemed then that great happiness
could be measured with the precision
of sharp pain. Quick and bitter.

Slow and sweet were the nights.
Now is as bitter and grinding as sand—
"We shall be sensible" and similar curses.

And as we stray further from love
we multiply the words,
words and sentences long and orderly.
Had we remained together
we could have become a silence.

Luxury

My uncle is buried at Sheik Bad'r.
The other one is scattered in the Carpathian mountains.

My father is buried at Sanhedria,
my grandmother on the Mount of Olives.
And all their forefathers
are buried in the ruined Jewish cemeteries in the villages of
    Lower Franconia,
near rivers and forests which are not Jerusalem.

My father's father kept heavy-eyed
Jewish cows in their sheds below the kitchen—

and rose at four in the morning.
I inherited his early rising,
my mouth bitter with nightmares
I attend to my bad dreams.

Grandfather, Grandfather,
Chief Rabbi of my life,
as you sold leavened bread on the Passover Eve,
sell my pains—
so they stay in me, even ache—but not mine,
not my property.

So many tombstones are scattered behind me—
names, engraved like the names of long-abandoned railway
    stations.

How shall I cover all these distances,
how can I keep them connected?
I can't afford such an intricate network.
It's a luxury.

Two Songs of Peace

1

My son smells of peace when I lean over him.
It isn't just the soap.
Everybody was once the child with the smell of peace.
(And in the whole country there isn't a single windmill which
    turns.)

O torn country, like torn clothes
which can't be mended,
and hard, lonely forefathers in Hebron's grave
in childless silence.

My son smells of peace.
His mother's womb
promised him that
which God can't promise us.

2

My love was not in the war.
She learns love and history
off my body, which was in two, or three.
And at night.
When my body makes battles into peace
she is bewildered.
Her perplexity is her love. And her learning.
Her wars and her peace, her dream.

And I am now in the middle of my life.
The time when one begins to collect
facts, and many details,
and exact maps
of a country we shall never occupy
and of an enemy and lover
whose borders we shall never cross.

My Child

When I last saw my child
he ate only porridge.
Now he's sad.

He eats bread and meat with a fork and knife
and with manners, which already prepare him
to die politely, and quietly.

He thinks that I'm a sailor,
but knows I have no ship.
And that we have no sea.
Only vast distances, and winds.

My father's movements in prayer
and my own in love
lie already folded in his small body.

To be grown-up is
to bake the bread of longing,
to sit the whole night long
with a reddening face
opposite the open oven.

My child sees everything.

And that magic spell "See you,"
which he's learned to say,
is only valid among the dead.

Song of Resignation

1

I resign!

My son has my father's eyes,
my mother's hands,
and my own mouth.
There is no further need of me. Many thanks.
The refrigerator is beginning to hum towards a long journey.
An unknown dog sobs over the loss of a stranger.

2

I resign!

I paid my dues to so many funds.
I am fully insured.
Let the world care for me now;
I am knotted and tied with it and all of them.
Every change in my life will cost them cash.
Every movement of mine will hurt them,
my death will dispossess them.
My voice passes with clouds,
my hand, stretched out, has turned into paper. Yet another contract.
I see the world through the yellow roses
someone has forgotten
on the table near my window.

3

Bankruptcy!
I declare the whole world to be a womb.
And as of this moment
I appoint myself,
order myself
at its mercy.
Let it adopt me. Let it care for me.

I declare the President of the United States to be my father,
the Chairman of the Soviet Union to have my power of attor-
      ney,
the British Cabinet to be my family,
and Mao Tse-tung to be my grandmother.

I resign!

I declare the heavens to be God:
They all together go ahead and do those things
that I never believed they would.

To My Mother

1

Like an old windmill,
two hands always raised
to howl at the sky
and two lowered
to make sandwiches.

Her eyes are clean and glitter
like the Passover eve.

2

At night she will put
all the letters
and the photographs
side by side.

So she can measure
the length of God's finger.

3

I want to walk in the deep
wadis between her sobs,
I want to stand in the terrible heat
of her silence.

I want to lean on the
rough trunks
of her pain.

4

She laid me
as Hagar laid Ishmael
under one of the bushes.

So that she won't have to be at my death
in the war,
under one of the bushes
in one of the wars.

Mayor

It's sad
to be the Mayor of Jerusalem.
It is terrible.
How can any man be the mayor of a city like that?

What can he do with her?
He will build, and build, and build.

And at night
the stones of the hills round about
will crawl down
towards the stone houses,
like wolves coming
to howl at the dogs
who have become men's slaves.

My Father Fought Their War for Four Years

My father fought their war for four years
and he didn't hate his enemies or love them.
But I know that even there
he formed me daily out of his little calms,
so rare; he gathered them out of the bombs
and the smoke,
and he put them in his frayed knapsack
with the last bits of his mother's hardening cake.

And with his eyes he gathered nameless dead;
he gathered many dead on my behalf,
so that I will know them in his look and love them.

And not die, like them, in horror . . .

And he filled his eyes with them in vain:

I go out to all my wars.

The United Nations' Command in Jerusalem

The mediators, the peace makers, the compromisers, the pacifiers
live in the white house
and receive their nourishment from far away,
through twisting channels, through dark veins, like a foetus.

And their secretaries are lipsticked and laughing,
and their immune chauffeurs wait below, like horses in a stable,
and the trees whose shadow shades them have their roots in dis-
     puted territory,
and the delusions are children who go out into the fields to find
     cyclamen
and do not come back.

And the thoughts circle above, uneasily, like scout planes,
and they take photographs, and return, and develop the film
in dark, sad rooms.

And I know that they have very heavy chandeliers,
and the boy that I was sits on them and swings
in and out, in and out, and out, and does not come back.

Later on, the night will bring
rusty and crooked conclusions out of our ancient lives,
and above all the houses the music
will gather all the scattered things,
like a hand gathering crumbs off the table
after the meal while the talk continues
and the children are already asleep.

And hopes come to me like daring sailors,
like discoverers of continents
to an island,
and they rest for a day or two,
and then they sail away.

You Also Were So Tired

You also were so tired of being an advertisement for
the world, for the angels to admire. It's lovely here.
Take a rest from smiling. And without complaint,
let the sea wind pleat your mouth.

You won't mind, like flying paper
your eyes also fly; fruit also dropped off the sycamore.
How does one say "to love" in the language of water?
What are we in the language of earth?

Here is the road and the going on it, what does it mean?
Whatsoever hill, the Last Wind. Which prophet. . . ?
And at night, out of my sleep you speak.
And how shall I answer, and what shall I bring?

Two Bedouin Songs

1
HE LIVES IN A HOUSE IN THE CITY

Buttons fall away, one by one,
Not in battles, not in rape—
From time to time they jump off in little explosions.
A dry sob of trousers and shirts.

Across the wall a yellow woman
Teaches children to play the guitar and a harmonica.
I provide her
With the dry air, the longing air for harmonicas.

Against my will
the barber cuts off a black straggling hair growing in my nose
extinguishing the rage,
castrating the fury
in my nose.

And in the nights
moonlight pierces through the crack in the letter box,
lights it,
white
like a letter.

2
HE LOVES

No house would have us.

I stretched myself above you, like a tent,
I spread myself beneath you,
a straw mattress.

128

Your red dress opened up heavenwards,
like a goblet—
you sat on me upright
to keep your thighs off the hard ground.

"Madman," you said in your strange language.

His dog died in his chains.
His friends remote—
his son dreams the saying of Kaddish.

Indian Summer in Princeton

Indian summer is a Jewish summer.
Your eyes are so heavy they almost fall out—
held back, they are, by the sadness of your face.
They do not fall out because of dryness,
and the forgetting of the fruit,
But because of the weight of the remembering.
The ground beneath us moves further away—
this falling away will go on,
and go on.

It was Sunday, their Sabbath,
time to sit down and ask ourselves
whom we really love.
In the house lives someone whose name is not the same as the
      name on the gate—
a woman told me that she does not love her life
and which of the trees are sick, just as people are sick.

But in my dreams I look at bright, blinding Jerusalem—
and that's why Jerusalem's black now,
like an underexposed photograph.

The Heart Is a Corrupt Director

The last days of summer
are the last days of two, together.

The heart is a corrupt director.

Departing departs from departing.
And in the nights it is written:
despair which despaired of us
became hope.

I think that even Newton discovered
whatever he discovered
in the lull between
one pain and another.

What bearing could this have
on the headiness of our lives?
What bearing on the soft talk
which surrounds them?
What manner of things have to fall
from which tree, for us to learn?

It is terrible to battle against love
with sleeping pills. What have we come to!

National Thoughts

You: trapped in the homeland of the Chosen People.
On your head a cossack's fur hat,
child of their pogroms.
"After these words." Always.

130

Or, for instance, your face: slanting eyes,
Pogrom Year eyes. Your cheekbones, high,
Hetman's cheekbones, Hetman the rabble king.
Hassid dancing, dutiful, you, naked on a rock in the early eve-
    ning by the canopies of water at Ein Geddi
with eyes closed and your body open like hair.

After these words, "Always."
Every day I know the miracle of
Jesus walking upon the waters,
I walk through my life without drowning.

To speak, now, in this tired language
torn from its sleep in the Bible—
blinded, it lurches from mouth to mouth—
the language which described God and the Miracles,
says:
motor car, bomb, God.

The squared letters wanted to stay closed,
every letter a locked house,
to stay and to sleep in it forever.

If I Forget Thee, Jerusalem

If I forget thee, Jerusalem,
then let my right be forgotten.
Let my right be forgotten, and my left remember.
Let my left remember, and your right close
and your mouth open near the gate.

I shall remember Jerusalem
And forget the forest—my love will remember,
will open her hair, will close my window,
will forget my right,
will forget my left.

If the west wind does not come
I'll never forgive the walls,
or the sea, or myself.
Should my right forget,
my left shall forgive,
I shall forget all water,
I shall forget my mother.

If I forget thee, Jerusalem,
Let my blood be forgotten.
I shall touch your forehead,
forget my own,
my voice change
for the second and last time
to the most terrible of voices—
or silence.

Rain on a Battlefield

It rains on my friends' faces,
on my live friends' faces,
those who cover their heads with a blanket.
And it rains on my dead friends' faces,
those who are covered by nothing.

The First Battles

The first battles raised
Terrible love flowers
With almost killing kisses
Like shells.
The boy soldiers
are driven in our city's handsome buses:
Number 12, number 8, and number 5 go to the front.

High-Heeled Shoes

The earth answered several times:
Come in!
When you crossed the road in your tapping
high-heeled shoes,
it said, Come in!
But you couldn't hear.

They Call Me

Taxis below
and angels above
are impatient.
At one and the same time
they call me
with a terrible voice.

I'm coming, I am
coming,
I'm coming down,
I'm coming up!

It's a Long Time Since Anybody's Asked

It's a long time since anybody's asked
who lived in these houses, and who last spoke; who
forgot his overcoat in these houses,
and who stayed. (Why didn't he run away?)

A dead tree stands among the blossoming trees. A dead tree.
It's an old mistake, never understood,
and at the edge of the country; the beginning
of somebody else's time. A little silence.
And the ravings of the body and hell.
And the end of the end which moves in whispers.
The wind passed through this place
and a serious dog watched humans laugh.

Time

translated by Yehudi Amichai

1

Songs of continuity, land mines and graves.
These are turned up when you build a house or a road:
Then come the black crow people from Meah Sh'earim*
to screech bitterly "dead, dead." Then come
young soldiers and with hands still bare from last night
they dismantle iron and decipher death.

So come, let's build no house and pave no road!
Let's make a house folded up in the heart
and a road rolled up in a coil in the soul, inside,
and we shall not die forever.

People here live inside prophecies that came true
as inside a thick cloud after an explosion
that did not disperse.
And so in their lonely blindness they
touch each other between the legs, in the twilight,
for they have no other time and they
have no other place,
and the prophets died long ago.

*Meah Sh'earim—Quarter of the ultra-orthodox in Jerusalem.

2

At the monastery of Latroun, in expectation of wine
being wrapped for me in the cool house,
there fell upon me all the laziness
of this land: holy, holy, holy.

I lay in the dry grass, on my back,
I saw high summer clouds in the sky,
motionless, like me below.
Rain in another land, peace in my heart.
And from my penis white seeds will fly
as from a dandelion tuft.
(Come, blow: poof, poof.)

3

On this evening I think again
about many days
that have sacrificed themselves
for just one night of love.
I think about this waste and this waste's fruit,
about abundance and about fire
and how without pain—time.

I've seen roads leading from one man
to another woman.
I've seen a life blurred
like a letter in the rain.
I've seen a dining table on which
things were left,
and wine on which was written, "The Brothers,"
and how without pain—time.

4

My son was born in a hospital called Assuta.*
Since then I have watched
his life as much as I could.

My son, when schools leave you
and you are left bare and vulnerable,
when you see life being torn
at its edges, and the world
falling apart at the joints, come again to me:
I'm still a great expert
on bewilderment and calm.

I'm like a peaceful album
with its photographs torn out
or just fallen out by themselves.
It has lost almost nothing of its weight.
So I have stayed the same man,
almost without memories.

*Assuta—a hospital in Tel-Aviv.

5

The bodies of two lovers hurt
after rolling all day long in the grass.

Their lying-awake-together at night
brings salvation to the world,
but not to them.

A bonfire burning in the open field
repeats blind with pain
the sun's work during the day.

Childhood is far away.
War is near. Amen.

6

The soldiers in the grave say: You above
who place wreaths on us,
like a life preserver made of flowers,
regard our faces so alike
between the outstretched arms. But
remember the difference there was between us
and the joy on the surface of the water.

7

In each buying and each loving
something has remained of our
Father Abraham's biblical wisdom,
when he bought a beautiful and cool
cave-tomb, while still alive,
to stay forever and remember.
That's the way to love in this land
and that's the way to buy.

And on Lag Be'omer* people get
married and make bonfires.
The smell of burning is in the air
together with the perfume of brides
Rabbis carry folded wedding canopies
on their shoulders like stretchers
to be used again and again
on this day.

And children carry bows and arrows
to play until it's a real war.
That's the way to fight wars.

And that's the way to remember in this land,
in which childhoods are far away from people
like times before the destruction of the temple.

They have a "Book of Children, One"
and a "Book of Children, Two"
like the "Book of Kings, One" and the
"Book of Kings, Two" in the Bible.

*Lag Be'omer—a memorial day in summer on which bonfires and many weddings are
held.

8

This is my mother's house. The plant
which started to climb on it
in my childhood has grown since and
clings to its wall. But I was
torn away long ago.

140

Mother, in pain you gave birth to me,
in pain lives your son.
His sadness is combed and groomed,
his happiness well dressed.
With his dream he earns his bread
and with his bread his dream.
The average annual rainfall
does not touch him
and degrees of temperature will
pass by him in weeping shade.

Oh my mother, who presented
me with a first welcome drink
in this world: L'haim, l'haim,*
my son!
I haven't forgotten a thing, but my life
has become calm and deep
like a second gulp deep in the throat,
not like the first one, with sucking
smacking, happy lips.

Your steps on the stairs
have always stayed in me,
never coming nearer and never going away,
like heartbeats.

*L'haim—"To your health!" in Hebrew.

9

What's this? This is an old
toolshed.
No, this is a great past love.

Anxiety and Joy were here together
in this darkness
and Hope.
Perhaps I've been here once before.
I didn't go near to find out.

These are voices calling out of a dream.
No, this is a great love.
No, this is an old toolshed.

10

No eye has ever seen,
nor any ear heard,
no bird has ever told it:
This child, sleeping, like a compass needle
trembling slightly at night.
But his head doesn't
move, secure in the holy ark
of his father's worry.

No eye has ever seen,
no dream ever dreamt
no mouth ever spoken this child.

In ancient times they used to say:
"Loved, like the apple of his eye." What, what,
like the apple of his eye? This child.
What is the apple of an eye? A ball made
from tears and paint.

Oh, all my words, sad
and happy nails of my life.

11

"How beautiful are thy tents, Jacob."
Even now, when there are neither tents nor Jacob's
tribes, I say, how beautiful.

Oh, may there come something of redemption,
an old song, a white letter,
a face in the crowd, a door opening
for the eye, multicolored
ice cream for the throat,
oil for the guts, a warm
memory for the breast.

Then my mouth will open wide
in everlasting praise,
open like the belly of a
wide-open calf hung on a hook
in a butcher's shop of the Old City market.

12

Advice for good love: Don't love
those from far away. Take yourself one
from nearby.
The way a sensible house will take
local stones for its building,
stones which have suffered in the same cold
and were scorched by the same sun.
Take the one with the golden wreath
around her dark eye's pupil, she
who has a certain knowledge
about your death. Love also inside

ruins like taking honey out of
the lion's carcass that Samson killed.

And advice for bad love: With
the love left over
from the previous one
make a new woman for yourself,
then with what is left of that woman
make again a new love,
and go on like that
until nothing remains for you.

13

Shifra and Batia promised
with their hips eternal youth.

Their dates of birth, still so fresh,
fill their thighs with sweet tension
and my brain with a golden sound like a light
     string.

They said: Aren't men weird and crazy
to decorate a sword made to kill
with beautiful carvings and precious stones,
but the penis, which is all made for joy,
they don't decorate.

14

This girl, halfway through high school,
brings back to me lost things
without knowing it herself.
I don't know her name, but
she is so beautiful that I feel happy
not to be her father, and not her god.

Will we still love her even
when they cut away from her body
a leg or a hand, an ear or the nose?

Her belly is still a soft botanical belly
not hard like bellies of man-eating evil women.
Her eyes are clear without mist of generations.
In her smooth hair there still remains
like some imprint of a wreath of flowers
a memory from a harvest dance in school
in her childhood.

Will we still love her
when they chop off
more and more
until nothing is left of her
but a basketful of girl,
a basketful of you?

15

I passed a house where I once lived:
A man and a woman are still together in the whispers.
Many years have passed with the silent buzz
of staircase bulbs—on, off, on.

The keyholes are like small delicate wounds
through which all the blood has oozed out
and inside people are pale as death.

I want to stand once more as in my
first love, leaning on the doorpost
embracing you all night through, standing.
When we left at early dusk the house
started to crumble and collapse
and since then the town
and since then the whole world.

I want once more to have this longing
until dark red burn marks show in the skin.

I want once more to be written
in the book of life, to be written
anew every day
until the writing hand hurts.

16

People on this shore will never again
step into the footprints which
they left in the sand
while last passing here.

This is a weeping truth
but sometimes it weeps
out of happiness
about the world being so wide
that there is no need to come back
to the same places.
Everything is up in heaven.

Toward evening I saw
a tanned lifeguard
bending over a golden rescued woman
reviving her with his breath,
like lovers.

17

To my love, while combing her hair
without a mirror, facing me,
a psalm: You've washed your hair
with shampoo: A whole pine forest
breathes on your head in nostalgia.

Calmness from inside and calmness from outside
have hammered your face
between them like copper.

The pillow on your bed is your auxiliary brain
folded under your neck for memory and dream.

The earth trembles beneath us, my love.
Let's lie together, a double safety lock.

18

"One sees all kinds of things," said the Swedish
officer observing at the armistice line.
"All kinds of things," and said nothing more.

"One sees a lot of things," said the old
shoeshine man by the Jaffa gate
when a Swedish girl in a very short dress
stood above him, without looking at him
with her proud eyes.

The prophet who looked into the opening heaven saw,
and so did God, "all kinds of things" down there
      beyond the smoke,
and the surgeon saw when he cut open a cancerous
      belly
and closed it again.

"One sees all kinds of things," said
our ancestor Jacob on his bed after the blessing
which took his last strength. "All kinds
of things," and he turned
toward the wall and he died.

19

How did a flag come into being?
Let's assume that in the beginning
there was something whole, which was
then torn into two pieces, both big enough
for two battling armies.

Or like the ragged striped fabric
of a beach chair in an abandoned
little garden of my childhood,
flapping in the wind. This
too could be a flag making you arise
to follow it or to weep at its side,
to betray it or to forget.

I don't know. In my wars
no flag-bearer marched in front
of the gray soldiers in clouds of dust and smoke.
I've seen things starting as spring,
ending up with hasty retreat
in pale dunes.
I'm now far away from all that, like one
who in the middle of a bridge
forgets both its ends
and remains standing there
bent over the railing
to look down into the streaming water:
This too is a flag.

20

The diameter of the bomb was thirty centimeters
and the diameter of its effective
range—about seven meters.
And in it four dead and eleven wounded.
And around them in a greater circle
of pain and time are scattered
two hospitals and one cemetery.
But the young woman who was
buried where she came from
over a hundred kilometers away
enlarges the circle greatly.
And the lone man who weeps over her death
in a far corner of a distant country
includes the whole world in the circle.
And I won't speak at all about the crying of orphans
that reaches to the seat of God
and from there onward, making
the circle without end and without God.

21

The figure of a Jewish father I am
with a sack on my back returning
home from the market. I have a rifle hidden
among soft woman-things in the closet in the scent
    of lingerie.
A man hit by the past and ill with future I am.
The fever of the present in his reddened eyes
unpaid and in vain he stands guard against evil.

Useless he guards against death,
guarding Jewish flesh, sweet like
all hunted flesh in agony. And at evening
he hears church bells rejoicing at the plight of Jews.
And from the hills a sad maneuver of brigades
with guns that have roots instead of wheels.
And he buys himself cream
for his cracked boots and his cracked lips.
And he smears it on for healing and for peace.

And he has documents of mercy and
papers of love in his coat.
And he sees people in their haste hurrying from past
    into future.
And at night, lonely and slowly he cooks jam,
stirring round and round till it grows pulpy and dense
with thick bubbles like thick Jewish eyes
and froth, white and sweet for coming generations.

22

What's that? That's an airplane at
daybreak. No, they are digging a sewer
up there. No, this is a deep
rift running along this wonderful nightingale.
No, this is a violent tearing sexual orgy
between a male and a female bulldozer.
No, this is the screech of a peacock:
This beautiful bird utters such a bitter scream.
But this is a silent song of praise.

No, these are words of comfort
for mourners, humming like
a kettle on a dying fire. But
this, surely, was an explosion!
No, this was a hollow and very heavy nightingale.
This sounds like night. No, this
was a lark announcing the new day.
This is the sunrise of nations.
No, this is my friend, the quiet cannonier,
whistling and feeding his domestic cannons
with shells at early dawn.

What's this? This is a misunderstanding of love:
Don't be frightened, child, this dog
loves you. He only wants to play with you.
Just a misunderstanding of love,
like our tears at the old window
overlooking the valley.

23

Sons of warm wombs join the army.
Those with feet kissed by mothers and aunts
and with shoes decorated with buckles and
        beautiful buttons
will have to pass through minefields.

Their eyelashes, glory of their beauty,
will become a double fence,
letting no one in and no one out.

Oh, what bar-mitzvahs* will they have,
what good deeds, what wedding parties!

Therefore, mothers, make round sons
round without hard joints,
make them like balls
that won't get hurt, just bounce
and bounce and bounce.

*bar mitzvah—Jewish confirmation of boys at the age of 13.

24

When my head got banged on the door, I screamed,
"My head, my head." And I screamed, "Door, door."
And I did not scream, "Mother," and not, "God."
Nor did I speak of the vision of the End of Days
of a world where there will be no heads and doors
        anymore.

When you stroked my head I whispered,
"My head, my head," and I whispered, "Your hand, your
        hand."
And I did not whisper, "Mother," and not, "God."
And I did not see wonderful visions
of hands stroking heads in the wide-opening heavens.

Whatever I scream and speak and whisper is
to comfort myself: My head, my head.
Door, door. Your hand, your hand.

25

"Sometime before his death," that's
what I overheard once while
passing two people standing at the traffic light.

As when someone leaves you
and enters into a dream
never to come out again.

Or when you put out
the lights of a big chandelier
with many bulbs
and you have to switch off all of them
and then go once more through all the stages
of light:
small light, big light,
and only after that, darkness.

26

This garden with your confession in it:
"Destroyed by love," you said
and other things which I've forgotten.

But I remember the tops of the trees
already darkening above
while the words below were still in light.

And there is a window
and he who opened it
will never be the one to close it.

And there is a number
on the door of a house
which was marked into my heart
like a number branded into a horse's skin.

"Destroyed by love." And other last
voices which have since
become food for birds and little animals of night.

27

The old ice factory in Petah-Tikvah:*
a wooden tower, boards blackened by rot.
In my childhood a weeping lived there.
I remember the tears
dripping from board to board
to still the summer's rage
and make ice below
which slid out of a deep opening.

And immediately, behind the dark cypresses,
they started to talk! "You live
only once."

I didn't understand then
and now that I understand, it's too late.

The cypresses are just as they were
and the water goes on
dripping somewhere else.

*Petah Tikvah—old village in Israel.

28

I heard talking outside my window:
a woman like a dove, a dove, a dove.
So I said in my heart: My two sons
are so far from each other, so far
in time, in place, and in mother.

My world is all mixed up: the tears
astray in my throat, my ear, my nose.

There, on that balcony, I was once loved.
Now the plants have grown and cover it all.

I'm outside. I'm a clock-hand
which has run away from its clock
but cannot forget its circling movement.

When I go straight toward my endless end
it hurts, because I only know how to go round.

29

I've filtered out of the Book of Esther the residue
of vulgar joy, and out of the Book of Jeremiah
the howl of pain in the guts. And out of the
Song of Songs the endless search for love,
and out of the Book of Genesis the dreams
and Cain, and out of Ecclesiastes
the despair and out of the Book of Job—Job.
And from what was left over I pasted for myself a new
    Bible.
Now I live censored and pasted and limited and in peace.

156

A woman asked me last night in the darkened street
about the well-being of another woman
who had died before her time, and not in anyone's time.
Out of great tiredness I answered her:
She's fine, she's fine.

30

My friend, the things you do now
some years ago, I did.
The number of years I'm older than you
is the time that has passed since.

You can see now, hard-eyed and soft-necked.
My penis is the last bridgehead
thrust into a new generation of young women.

After this comes the removal
of love's remnants and rubbish of joy
like that of any annoying and hampering garbage.

I can see you grasping
desperately at all that surrounds you,
books, children, a woman,
musical instruments—
but you don't know that this
is nothing but pulling
dry twigs and dead branches to your body
for the big fire
in which you'll burn.

31

I've already been weaned from Adam's, the first man's,
    curse.
The twisting fiery sword is far away,
blazing in the sun like a propellor.
I already love the salty taste of the sweat of my brow
on my bread, together with dust and death.

But still the soul I was given
is like a tongue
that remembers sweet tastes.

I am already the second man. And they are already
chasing me out of the garden of curses
in which I settled down after the garden of Eden.

Now beneath my feet there grows for me
a small cave, fitted perfectly to the shape of my body.
I am a man of shelter: the Third Man.

32

When I was young the land was young
and my own father was everyone's father.
When I was happy the land was happy too.
And when I jumped on the ground, the ground
jumped under my feet. And the grass that covered it
    in spring
softened me too. Its dry hard soil in summer
hurt the cracked skin of my own feet.

When I had my great love
they declared my land's liberation.
When my hair flew in the wind, so did its flags.
When I fought, it had wars.
When I rose, it rose up. And when
I sank it started sinking with me.

Now I come apart from all this
like something that was glued, when the glue dries out.
I detach myself and curl into myself.

Not long ago I saw a clarinet player
in the Police Band, playing at the Tower of David.
His hair was white, his face peaceful.
The face of 1946—that one year
between famous and terrible years, a year
in which nothing at all happened—
only a great hope, and his music,
and my sleeping with a girl in a quiet
room in Jerusalem's nights.
I had not seen him since then,
but hope for a better world has not
left his face to this day.

After that I bought myself
some nonkosher sausage
and two bagels and went home
I ate and lay down on my bed
but the memory of my first love
came back to me
like the sudden sensation of falling
before sleep.

33

Listen, my old teacher: Life
is not deep as you taught us, history
and loves, Buber and Marx are
nothing but a thin skin of asphalt road
on this huge earth.

Oh, my teacher, the limit of toys is so near:
When a gun really kills and father is really dead.

And the limit of camouflage
which is also the limit of love:
Instead of a cannon there grows a real tree
and you become me
and I become you.

34

The door opened by mistake:
"You shouldn't be here now."

A thin whistle in the dark:
This was a young fig tree.

A slight despair lifted its head for a moment
like a watchdog and didn't even bark.

Rapists as in deep slumber in the forest
dreaming about real love.

"You shouldn't be here."
But here I am now.

Together we sailed to the sources of your madness:
a thundering waterfall. But in the morning
tranquil water.

35

In the garden at the white table
two dead men were sitting in the heat of day.
Above them, a branch moved slightly.
One of them pointed out things that never were,
the other spoke of a great love
with a special device to go on functioning
even after death.

It could be said they were
a cool and pleasant appearance
on this hot day, without sweat
and without voice. Only when they got up
I heard them like a ringing of porcelain
being removed from the table.

36

I'm like a leaf
knowing its limits,
not wanting to expand beyond
and not—
to become one with Nature
not to flow into the big world.

I'm so quiet now
I can't imagine
that I ever cried, even as a baby in pain.

My face is what is left
after they blasted it
and dug it for loves
like a stone quarry
now abandoned.

37

Karl Marx, cold and bitter one,
a man outside and a Jew in your grave in the foreign rain.
"Man lives by bread alone": yourself
bread alone, lonely bread that you are,
round loaf from the last century,
a loaf rolling and tumbling the whole world
upside down.

Here I am on this winter day in Jerusalem
where tired Jews search the bodies of passersby:
collarbones, breast, belly, crotch: danger and love.
My skin still protects me against the rain,
but in one of my tears, if I'm still weeping then,
there will remain something of this water
pouring down now from heaven.

Karl Marx, with a beard like a sage.
Ritual slaughterer of history
so that it can be clean and kosher, according to the Law.
Look, I have put a lamp in my window
to make a field of light for myself.
I pay my rent on time. This too
is some kind of defense line, but directly
in front of it the enemy's armies
are lined up with rockets and thunder,
last battle and first death
and nothing after.

Look, my love caresses my breast
which is the hairy side of my emotions.

Karl Marx, the last drop
will always be a tear.

38

A weeping mouth and a laughing mouth
in terrible battle before a silent crowd.

Each gets hold of the mouth, tears and bites
the mouth, smashes it to shreds and bitter blood.

Till the weeping mouth surrenders and laughs,
till the laughing mouth surrenders and weeps.

39

My child dreamt about me in his sleep
while I was dreaming about my father, may he rest in
	peace.

You have a living father and I—a dead one.
You start and I want to finish.

I'm far away from emotion and feeling
as coal is far away from the forest it was.

Your time too will turn into thin thread
and the sweet "tick" will separate from the "tock."

The game begins: No looking out of the window!
And he who remembers last—he wins.

40

"But what have you done for your soul?"
I slept a lot and also loved a lot,
unlike the tree which loves just once a year.
What a forest of crazy trees I am!

And then, what am I? At most
a transmitter of childhood memories
with high poles above the landscape
from afar to afar.
And for the sake of this humming,
And a few sparks, all this hard labor,
all this running, all this pain?

Finally everything is made according to man's
        measurements,
a hand, a foot, a finger's length. Even
a high house is nothing but a man
on top of a man, on top of a man.

"But what have you done for your soul?"

41

The evening lies along the horizon and donates blood.
Flights of birds move up the sky like black mist.

Love is a reservoir of tenderness and care
like the hoarding of food for times of siege.

A little boy sits upright in his bed.
His kingdom is eternal kingdom.

People put a fence around their house,
so that their hope will not be in vain.

In a white and closed room
a woman decides to grow her hair long again.

The earth is turned up for the seed.
A secret military installation blossoms in the dark.

42

These words, like heaps of feathers
on the edge of Jerusalem, above the Valley of the Cross.
There, in my childhood, the women sat
plucking chickens.
These words fly now all over the world.
The rest is slaughtered, eaten,
digested, decayed, forgotten.

The hermaphrodite of time
who is neither day nor night
has wiped out this valley
with green well-groomed gardens.
Once experts of love used to come here
to perform their expertise
in the dry grass of summer nights.

That's how it started.
Since then—many words, many loves,
many flowers
bought for warm hands to hold
or to decorate tombs.

That's how it started
and I don't know how it will end.
But still from beyond the valley,
from pain, and from distance
we shall forever go on calling out
to each other: "We'll change."

43

A song, a psalm, on Independence Day.
All of it so far off, but still remembered
like the echo of footsteps whose bodies
turned to dust of the desert long ago.
The sound of trumpets that I hear—
not for me anymore.
Even the warm breath inside the trumpets—
not for me anymore.
And the remembered dust has turned
into forgetting fields.

Builders and destroyers gather
in my house in the evening
to sit all night through on the balcony
watching the fireworks
which are the many-colored sighs of the Jewish people.

Come, let's not talk about the famous six million,
let's talk about just one of them—me:
I am a man like a dead mound.
But in each of my layers
something still moves.

44

The little park planted in memory of a boy
who fell in the war begins
to resemble him
as he was twenty-nine years ago.
Year by year they look more alike.
His old parents come almost daily
to sit on a bench
and look at him.

And every night the memory in the garden
hums like a little motor:
During the day you can't hear it.

45

On New Year's Day, next to a house being built,
a man vows not to do any wrong in it,
only to love in it.
Sins that were green in spring
have dried out in summer and now rustle and whisper.

So I washed my body and trimmed my fingernails—
the last favor
which a man does for himself
while he is still alive.

What is man? During the day
he breaks up into little words
what night has turned into a heavy lump.
What are we doing to each other?
What does a father do to his son?
What—a son to his father?

And nothing stands between
him and death
but a thin defense, like a battery
of excited lawyers,
a fence of words.

And he who uses people as handles, or as steps of a ladder,
will soon find himself
embracing a piece of wood
and holding a hand cut from its body
and wiping his tears
with a potsherd.

46

You carry the load of heavy buttocks,
but your eyes are clear.
Around your waist you wear a strong belt
which won't be able to protect you.

You are made of material that slows down
the process of joy and its pain.

I have already taught my penis
to say your name, like a clever bird.
You seem unimpressed by this,
you pretend not to hear it.
What else should I have done for you?

Now all that's left to me
is your name
which has become completely independent, like an animal:
It eats out of my hand and
lies down at night
curled up in my dark brain.

47

In the beginning there was great joy—
like the joy when two strangers meet.

Every night each one returns to his tunnel
to dig in it, alone.

In the morning there arrived the Non-Letter.

48

There came upon me a terrible longing
like people in an old photograph
who want to be back among the others
who are looking at them
in the good light of a lamp.

Here in the house I think
how love has turned into friendship
in the chemistry of our life.
I think about friendship which calms us for death
and how our lives are like single threads
without any hope of being rewoven
into another cloth.

Out of the desert
come muffled sounds,
dust prophesies dust, an airplane
fastens above our heads
the zipper of a huge bag of fate.

And the memory of a girl I once loved
moves along the valley tonight, like buses—
many lighted windows passing, many her-faces.

49

I am a man "planted beside streams of water,"
but I'm not "blessed be the man."
The desert is calm all around me, but there's no peace
    in me.

Two sons I have, one still small,
and whenever I see a child crying
I want to make another one
as if I hadn't got it right
and wanted to start afresh.
And my father is dead, and God is only one, like me.
And the Hill of Evil Counsel sails into the night
all covered with antennae up to heaven.

I'm a man planted beside streams of water,
but I can only weep it,
and sweat it, and urinate it
and spill it from my wounds—
all this water.

50

A song of friendship, while parting from a friend:
Now I shall extinguish my desert with your fat wet fields,
I shall drive deep into your green swamps
the burning sharp rocks of my country
like hot iron into eyes:
In hissing steam and in the white soothing vapor
again an old pain will unite us
and eternal joy will be on our heads.

Toward evening we stood once more together
in the field leaning to the river.
The smell of earth came up from beneath
and I said in my heart: like dung on the soil,
good blessed dung and silence.

Goodbye, my friend, go back to your house
with your heavy steps. The light of sunset
will also light windows of houses
where nobody lives anymore.

51

To a friend who is a priest: With sad
and soft eyes you once more, as in ancient
times, swing the pampered thighbone
for a burned offering,
and smoke your private incense
in your half-clogged pipe.
You refuse to degrade yourself to
the caste of blessing priests in synagogue
with wailing voice and cramped
fingers like those of old women
or to receive alms at rituals of firstborn males.

Lacking beautiful ceremonious attire you
sit wrapped in the folds of your own fat
in the Turkish Bath among
crude and hairy laymen.
But you are still sensitive, almost allergic,
to dead corpses and cemeteries: Your hair
stands on end like the hair of a cat
when you pass near something dead.
In the pockets of your baggy trousers
which you take out of the iron locker
in the dressing room
a bunch of keys rings like
the little bells in the ancient Temple.

One of the keys is very old, and
has lost its house,
so my friend the priest
can whistle on it
to call back brilliant memories
like whistling a dog.

52

Jerusalem is a cradle city rocking me.
Whenever I wake up strange things happen to me
in the middle of the day, as though to someone
descending the stairs of his love's house
for the last time, with eyes still closed.
But my days force me to open my eyes and
to remember everyone passing me: Perhaps
he'll love me, perhaps he has planted a bomb
wrapped in nice paper like a present of love.
I observe all the weak spots in these stone houses,
the crack though which electricity enters,
the hole pierced for waterpipes,
the cunt for telephone wires to penetrate
and the mouths of sighs.

I am a Jerusalemite. Swimming pools with
their voices and noises are no part of my soul.
The dust is my conscious, the stone my subconscious,
and all my memories are closed courtyards
at summer's high noon.

53

At an archeological site
I saw fragments of precious vessels, well cleaned
and groomed and oiled and spoiled.
And beside it I saw a heap of discarded dust
which wasn't even good for thorns and thistles
        to grow on.

I asked: What is this gray dust which
has been pushed around and shifted
and tortured and then thrown away?

I answered in my heart: This dust
is people like us, who during their
lifetime lived separated from
copper and gold and marble stones
and all other precious things—
and they remained so in death.
We are this heap of dust, our
bodies, our souls, all the words
in our mouths, all hopes.

54

Evening hours of the soul
are upon me already in the morning.

Soft footsteps on lush grass, like hope
for something. Shoes always remain hard.

A little child stands motionless in the field
without knowing that he is thus eternal.

A man with two futures weeps in sudden fear,
a man empty of memories fills up his body, so he
    won't drift away.

A woman reads a letter at her window,
and doing so she changes beyond recognition.

A door opens and closes and opens.
Another remains closed: beyond it—silence.

55

A snare flies up from the ground
with outspread wings, this summer night.

A computer rolls his eyes upward
like a happy martyred saint.

Hoarse girls lure men
to their outings with hoarse voices.

In a lighted house sweet lovers tear
each other to quiet blood-dripping rags.

In the garages of the Kidron Valley
a black hearse is being repaired.

An orphaned father seats his little son on his knees
and sings him a lullaby about his sins.

The eyes of the sleepers are mines,
the first light of day will set them off.

56

In Talpiot* the floors are slowly sinking.
All the tiles are tired eyelids of the earth
wanting nothing but sleep.

The windows of the old house
have remained only for looking inside:
the final destiny of all windows.

*Talpiot—old suburb of modern Jerusalem.

Once I knew a woman here, with dark velvet eyes,
who used to keep saying: "Look
how the light falls."

Much have I loved her and
much has she spoiled sights of
landscapes and of love. But the light
she spoke of is still falling
and, unlike her, is
still unshattered.

57

The cemetery of Messilat Zion* in the mountains
of Jerusalem, toward evening:
a sudden relief after the narrow valley.
The people were born in India and came by air and by sea,
now buried here. Their graves in disarray,
each one pointing in a different direction,
like boats scattered after the storm has passed.

A blue wooden fence which can contain nothing.
Soft things cover the hard worlds in spring.
The Luf flower grows half hidden and
reminds me of deep and terrible things in my life.

I ask myself: Does salvation grow out
of all this? Does salvation grow
at all? And what are its seeds?

*Messilat Zion—a village in the mountains.

58

This man crossing the field was once
a Chief Rabbi in Africa. And I
used to be the chief lover in my house.
In spite of his age he is making
a new future for himself with
serious excursions and walks into
the Judaean mountains. He is learning.
He observes one wisdom piling up
stones for a wall and another wisdom
scattering them again all over the field.
He also observes a burnt field
and he knows by now that a burnt field
can never be burned again.
This too is some kind of hope and great peace.

All this is very well known,
like the blowing wind or
like Rachel mourning her children
in her grave.

59

Early in the morning
you lean against the wall of an old house.
After that you jump lightly
onto a bus with all the other jumpers.

With holy shoes like these
you go daily to work in an office
with a love dress like this,
to open and to close.

What protects you? Very thin
stockings up to your navel.

What supports this old house?
A memory supports it, till
you come to lean against it
next morning.

60

The day olive trees breathed deeply
and the hills learned again to dance like lambs
I saw my son's face when I was alone.
I was so alone that I saw.
Sleep in me, said the landscape, sleep, sleep.

I saw birds flying up and birds flying down
as when people leave you
and others come in their stead.

I saw men sitting in their homes
crying: "I want to go home!"
with the calm faces of men sitting
in their homes.

Sleep in me, said the landscape, sleep, sleep.

61

With open eyes as only the dead have
I travel. A lust to see other countries,
which filled me in my youth, has gone
without satisfaction.
Accustomed to travel, I stop at every door
and turn round, to see again
if I forgot something—
so I lengthen my stay.

And now I wait for the great happiness:
When my old mother will pace inside my brain
truly, in flesh and blood, with a stooped walk,
will pace, to and fro
from ear to ear, inside my brain—this
will be my great happiness.

62

Departure from a place where you had no love
includes the pain of all that did not happen
together with the longing for what will happen
        after you leave.

On my last evening I saw on the floor
of the balcony across the street
a small and exact square of light
bearing witness to great emotions
which have no limits.

And when I went early in the gray morning
to the railway station
many people were passing me
carrying lists of wonderful strange names
which I'll never come to know,
postmen, tax collectors, municipal clerks
and others. Perhaps angels.

63

When a man has been away from his homeland a long time,
his language becomes more and more precise
less and less impure,
like precise clouds of summer
on their blue background
which will never rain.

Thus, all those who were once lovers
still speak the language of love, sterile
and clear, never changing, and never
getting any response.

But I, who have stayed here, dirty my mouth
and my lips and my tongue.
In my words there is garbage of soul
and refuse of lust and dust and sweat.
Even the water I drink in this dry land,
between screams and memories of love,
is urine recycled back to me
through complicated circuits.

64

I love these people in their strong house
in the high North. From their window
you can see ships on their proud voyage
to an even farther North.
And whatever does not pass this window
does not exist.

Many islands, and not one memory.
The forests stand in everlasting rains,
the fat fern fronds are the only clue
to ancient happenings which were better forgotten.
And in the clearing, wet leaves in the mud
are a bed for burning love, with white steam.

"I'm the soul of this landscape," said
the woman. And so said another one,
and another, and another.

65

The house, in which I had many thoughts
when I was young, fell to pieces.
And so my thoughts are at large in the world and
    endanger me now.

Therefore I roam about a lot and change houses
so they won't find me.
Between two questions,
Has he arrived? and, Is he still here?
I always slip away, to new places.

The way of all flesh I'll go: hunted,
caught, slaughtered, sold even before
being killed, made kosher with bitter salt,
cut and tortured,
a strange life I have
and a strange death too
and a strange grave
with engraving mistakes
on the headstone.

66

Late in life I came to you
filtered through many doors
reduced by stairs
till almost nothing remained of me.

You are such a surprised woman
living with half courage,
a wild woman wearing spectacles—
those elegant reins of your eyes.

"Things like to get lost and be
found again by others. Only
human beings love to find themselves,"
you said.

After that you broke your whole face
into two equal profiles: one
for the far distance, the other for me—
as a souvenir. And you went.

67

We walked together, you and I,
like Abraham and his son Isaac.
But although we were a man and a woman,
and although we did not go to the sacrifice,
the knowledge of things still to happen
and the ignorance of what will befall
were close together, like lovers.

After that jaws of suitcases gaped open
and it turned out that what
we thought would be a few days of separation
became forever.

But since then there have remained between us
signs and special marks
like those exchanged by people who don't know each
other
when they plan
to meet in places where they have never been.

68

Small and fragile you stand in the rain,
a small target for raindrops in winter
and for the dust in summer
and also for fragments of bombs all year round.
Your belly is weak, unlike the
taut flat skin of a drum.
Yours is the softness of the third generation.
Your grandfather, the pioneer, dried swamps.
But the revenge of those swamps falls on you,
filling you with sucking madness,
boiling and babbling in many colors.

What will you do now? You'll collect
loves like stamps. Some of them are duplicates
and some are damaged. No one will trade with you.
Your mother's curse crouches at your side
like an exotic bird. You resemble it.

Your room stays empty. But every night
your bed is made with a clean sheet.
That's hell's punishment for your bed:
no one sleeping in it, without
wrinkles, without a stain,
like the cursed sky in summer.

69

My son, in whose face there is already a sign
of eagle—
like a daring prefix to your life,
let me kiss you once more while you still love it,
softly, like this.
Before you become a hairy Esau of open fields
be for a little while
soft-skinned Jacob for my blind hands.

Your brain is well packed in your skull,
efficiently folded for life. Had it stayed
spread out you might have been happier,
a large sheet of happiness without memory.

I'm on my way from believing in God
and you're on your way toward it: This too
is a meeting point of a father and a son.

It's evening now. The earthball is cooling,
clouds that have never lain with a woman
pass overhead in the sky, the desert
starts breathing into our ears,
and all the generations
squeeze a bar mitzvah for you.

70

In this valley which many waters
carved out in endless years
so that the light breeze may now
pass through it to cool my forehead,

I think about you. From the hills I hear
voices of men and machines wrecking and building.

And there are loves which cannot
be moved to another place.
They must die at their place and in their time
like an old clumsy piece of furniture
that's destroyed together with
the house in which it stands.

But this valley is a hope
of starting afresh without having to die first,
of loving without forgetting the other love,
of being like the breeze
that passes through it now
without being destined for it.

71

"He left two sons," that's
what they say about someone
who died. Sometimes he is still alive.

The echo of a great love is like
the echo of a huge dog's barking
in an empty Jerusalem house
marked for demolition.

72

My ex-pupil has become a policewoman.
There she is, standing at the crossroads in town:
She opens a box made of metal,
like a box of perfumes and cosmetics,
and changes the colors of the traffic lights
    according to her mood.

Her eyes are a mixture of green, red and yellow.
Her hair is cut very short, like that of fresh street urchins.
In her high black shoes she leans against the box.
Her skirt is short and tight. I don't even dare
to imagine all the terrible glory at the upper
end of all this golden tan.

I don't understand anymore. I'm already lost.
When I walk the street whole legions
of young men and young women are
thrown against me in ever-growing waves.
They seem to have endless reserves.
And my pupil, the policewoman,
is unable to stop them:
She even joins them!

73

Such a male on a bald mountain in Jerusalem,
a scream pries open his mouth,
a wind tears at his cheeks and reins him in
like a bit in the mouth of an animal.

The message of his love: "Be fruitful and multiply"
is a messy business like sticky sweets
on a child's fingers—and attracts flies.
Or like a half-empty tube of shaving cream
crusted and split.
The threats of his love: On your back!
You with all your legs and trembling antennae!
Just wait, I'll drive it deep into you,
as far as your great grandchildren.
And she'll answer him: They will
bite you deep inside me,
they'll be a generation of tough
rodents, those last offspring!

"But a man is not a horse," said the old
cobbler while he was widening and softening
my new and hard shoes.
And suddenly I wept, because of so much
love being poured over me.

74

So I find myself always on the run
from blows and from pain,
from sweaty hands and from hard hits.
Most of my life in Jerusalem, a bad place
to evade all these. All my wars took
place in deserts among hard stones and sharp wounding
    gravel.

I never had the luck to have a war
in a cool green forest
or in a wavy battle at sea.

And so I am on the run, evasive like
a pathetic dancer amid hurled stones
and falling shells, between strong
hands and outstretched arms,
a very clumsy and heavily loaded
man I am on the run,
my whole body loaded down from head to toe,
on my shoulder a rifle, around my belly
an ammunition belt, on my head
heavy guilt, my feet in shoe-cages,
on my back the heavy yoke of family care,
and even my knees, moving up and down,
activate a terrible time-motor.

Only my penis is still free and happy,
no good for sword fights and no good
for any work, or even for hanging things on,
or for digging trenches.
Praise be to God that it is so. Even onto
God I've loaded praise.

And so, much too heavy, I'm
on the run till the last pain
causes me no more pain.

75

A bird at dawn is singing
with too strong a voice
prophesying a day of dry hot winds.

At noon the shutters are pulled down
against the burning sun.
Then my soul makes love to me
from behind, all along my back
and I'm unable to return
to work because of all this pleasure.

Toward evening, the so-called Present Situation
lifts itself up from the people and
hangs up there, in one piece, like a high canopy,
and the quantity
of all the water in the world is turned
into the quality
of one tear in the eye.

76

On the wall of a house on which
bricks were painted I saw
visions of God.

A sleepless night which makes pain in the heads of others
made flowers opening in my brain.

And he who was lost like a dog
will be found like a man and come back.

Love is not the last room:
There are others along
the long corridor that has no end.

77

My God, the soul
you gave me
is smoke—
from never-ending burnings
of memories of love.

The minute we are born
we start burning them
and so on
until the smoke
dies, like smoke.

78

Here on the ancient beach of Tantura I sit
in the sand with my sons and my sons' sons not yet born.
But they are assembled with me in my crouched squatting.
The happiness of the water equals the happiness of heaven.
And the waves' foam penetrates my mind and becomes
    clear there.

And my past's future is here and now in my rest.
I see children playing in the sand:
The happy ones always destroy and
the sad ones build again.
But the voices of both are stronger
than the sound of the breaking waves.

There on that hillock beside the railway tracks
an old concrete pillbox still stands.
Thorns cover it. Its iron died long ago,
but its shooting slits have become
real eyes, sometimes seeing
and sometimes weeping thin sand.

There I stood in the summer of 1942
facing the sea, guarding against the enemy
to protect the continuation of my life
to reach until this moment.
New enemies come now from the east,
but the same wind still nestles
in sleepless reddened eyes.

79

Now all the lifeguards have left for their homes.
The bay is closed and all of the sun's
last light is concentrated
in a fragment of glass,
like all life in the breaking eye of the dying.

A clean washed board is saved
from the fate of becoming furniture.

Half an apple and half a footprint
in the sand try to become together
a new whole thing.
A blackened box looks like a man asleep or dead.
But even God stopped here and did
not approach it to know the truth.
The one and only mistake and the
one and only right thing we do
both bring peace to a man's mind.
The balance sheets of good and bad
are being opened and pour slowly
into the tranquil world.

In the dim light of dusk, by the
rock pool, a few young people still
warm themselves with emotions
I once had in this place.
Inside the water the green stone
looks like it's dancing with the dead
fish in rippling waves.
A girl's face emerges from diving
with eyelashes like rays of the sun
resurrected for the night.

80

So I went down to the ancient harbor: Deeds
of human beings bring the sea closer,
other deeds push it farther away.
How can the sea know what they want, which pier clasps
as in love, and which pier rejects?

In the shallow water lies a Roman column.
But this is not its final place. Even if they
take it from here and set it in a museum
with a small explanation, even that will
not be its final place: It will go on falling
through floors and strata and other times.

But now a breeze blowing through the tamarisks
fans a last red glow in the cheeks of those sitting there
like embers of a dying bonfire. After that, night
    and whiteness.
The salt eats everything and I eat
salt, till it eats me too.
And what was given to me was again taken
from me and again given, and what was thirsty
has since quenched its thirst,
and what was quenched has found rest in death.